BLOCKCHAIN & CRYPTOCURRENCIES

Everything you need to know about Bitcoin, Monero, Dash, Litecoin, Ethereum & Ripple

Building a High Quality Marketplace for Crypto Data

Anshul Kaushik

B.Tech, M.S. BITS Pilani, Ph.D. Scholar

Computer Security Consultant, BITS Pilani Alumnus

KHANNA BOOK PUBLISHING CO. (P) LTD.

Publisher of Engineering and Computer Books

4C/4344, Ansari Road, Darya Ganj, New Delhi-110002

Phone : 011-23244447-48 **Mobile:** +91-9910909320

E-mail : contact@khannabooks.com

Website : www.khannabooks.com

Dear Readers,

To prevent the piracy, this book is secured with HIGH SECURITY HOLOGRAM on the front title cover. In case you don't find the hologram on the front cover title, please write us to at contact@khannabooks.com or whatsapp us at +91-99109 09320 and avail special gift voucher for yourself.

Specimen of Hologram on front Cover title:

Moreover, there is a SPECIAL DISCOUNT COUPON for you with EVERY HOLOGRAM.

How to avail this SPECIAL DISCOUNT:

Step 1: Scratch the hologram
Step 2: Under the scratch area, your "coupon code" is available
Step 3: Logon to www.khannabooks.com
Step 4: Use your "coupon code" in the shopping cart and get your copy at a special discount
Step 5: Enjoy your reading!

Price : ₹ 155.00

ISBN: 978-93-86173-72-0

Blockchain & Cryptocurrencies

by Anshul Kaushik

First Edition: 2019
Second Edition: 2023
Reprint: 2024

Published by:
Khanna Book Publishing Co. (P) Ltd.
Visit us at: **www.khannabooks.com**
Write us at: **contact@khannabooks.com**
CIN: U22110DL1998PTC095547

To view complete list of books, Please scan the QR Code: KPH

Printed in India.

PREFACE

Understand Bitcoin, Blockchains, and Cryptocurrency

"Antony helps us all clearly understand the mechanics of Bitcoin and Blockchain."

–**Rob Findlay**, Founder, Next Money

Blockchains and Cryptocurrencies are now topics of substantial impact that academia, practitioners and the IT industry need to contemplate, study, research, publish, innovate, exploit and adopt.

Blockchain and Cryptocurrency are quickly becoming mainstream in today's economy and business practices. With this book, you can jump ahead of the curve and quickly understand what they are and how they are used.

If you are a management or business management student, you must have come across the terms *Blockchain* and *Cryptography.* But have you stopped to consider why businesses all over the world are going crazy about this technology?

The simple answer is that no one wants to miss the bus, and every business is looking forward to gaining a lot from their use. It's the new frontier of opportunity for those familiar with the territory.

Imagine a world without any printed currency, without passport, without any government. Issue licenses and certificates of your qualifications from the government. A life without physical banks and bank accounts. How does this sound?

It might look strange but we are moving towards this kind of world with the introduction of blockchain technology. Fifty years from now and it can become a reality.

There's a lot written on Cryptocurrency and Blockchains. But, for the uninitiated, most of this information can be indecipherable. The Basics of Bitcoins and Blockchains provides a clear guide to this new currency and the revolutionary technology that powers it.

Bitcoin, Ethereum, and other Cryptocurrencies. Gain an understanding of a broad spectrum of Bitcoin topics including the history of Bitcoin, the Bitcoin Blockchain, and Bitcoin buying, selling, and mining. Learn how payments are made, and how to put a value on cryptocurrencies and digital tokens.

Blockchain Technology. What exactly is a blockchain, how does it work, and why is it important? The Basics of Bitcoins and Blockchains answers these questions and more. Learn about notable blockchain platforms, smart contracts, and other important facets of blockchains and their function in the changing cyber-economy.

Things to know before buying Cryptocurrencies. Find trustworthy and balanced insights into Bitcoin investing and investing in another cryptocurrency. Discover the risks and mitigations, learn how to identify scams, and understand cryptocurrency exchanges, digital wallets, and regulations.

You might have heard about the bitcoin or any kind of Cryptocurrency from your friends or family. Also, there are many reports of bitcoin published frequently in major dailies across India. Bitcoin is also a social media buzzword which is often encountered while the browsing Internet on computer or mobile devices. It's also being publicized aggressively on Facebook & Twitter.

But you have wonderful that how this Bitcoin Cryptocurrency works? How this bitcoin system can exist as a self-automated system which is becoming popular day by day. Whether or not you want to invest in Bitcoin or want to know how it works. Blockchain Technology and Bitcoin is certainly interesting to learn about. Though in this book we are focused on Bitcoin because of its popularity as a Cryptocurrency but also you will find popular Cryptocurrencies and Bitcoin alternatives which personally, we think can surpass the current Bitcoin system in future.

This book will provide solid grounding for the Blockchain Technology and will take you on a slightly technical but interesting journey to the world of Blockchain and its associated applications.

You must be wondering why a single book on Blockchain and Bitcoin? The answer is that it is essential to understand Blockchain and Bitcoin? The answer is that it is essential to understand Blockchain to understand Bitcoin because Blockchain Technology is the super structure foundation on which most of the cryptocurrencies are build. Bitcoin as a Cryptocurrency is one of the application usages of Blockchain Technology.

We have encountered many people in conferences /session chairs who consider Blockchain and Bitcoin as a single thing but actually they are different. Both the things are very well connected but certainly they cannot be used in place of each other. In this book we are taking a combined approach to understand its functioning.

This book is divided into seven various sections. The first section of the book deals with the explanations of basic computing concepts that are required to understand the technology appropriately. We have taken several metaphors from day-to-day life to explain the complex topics with simplicity. The second section of the book explains the Blockchain Technology and how this technology became the foundation of Bitcoin and Cryptocurrency.

In the third section we will take Bitcoin Cryptocurrency in detail and will understand its used, investments, mining pools etc.

The fourth section deals with the other popular Cryptocurrencies and how they are different from Bitcoin. In this section we will also discuss the popular contenders of Bitcoin Cryptocurrency.

In fifth section we will try to understand the current legislations and legal aspect of using and investing in Cryptocurrency generally worldwide.

The sixth section is dedicated to the practical applications of Bitcoin and deals with the various methods of creating, investing and using Bitcoin as a global currency. The section helps the readers as step-by-step guide for creating wallets and engaging in transactions.

The last section of the book covers the important tables and list of various websites that are important tables and list of various websites that are important for Bitcoin in general. This section also contains some important tables and data related legality status in various countries including some important lists if podcasts to listen and other list websites.

It is strictly recommended that reader should read this book in chronological order. Moreover, this book is written for the normal average users who want to learn about the application, uses and working of Blockchain and Cryptocurrencies in general. Therefore, every concept is explained with metaphors where ever possible and obstinate algorithms and programming is generally avoided.

After reading this book we are sure that you will be more comfortable with the Blockchain and Bitcoin world and can carry out operations related to all Cryptocurrencies in general.

Hope you enjoy reading this first edition as much as I did in writing it!

Author

ACKNOWLEDGEMENT

No one walks alone and when one is walking on the journey of life just where we start to thank those who joined us, walked besides us, and helped us along the way.

Over the years, those that we have met and worked with have continuously motivated us to write this book. So, at last, here it is. So, perhaps this book and its pages will be seen as "thanks" to the tens of thousands of you who have helped bringing out this book in the form what is today.

There was, in and always will be the love of my students whom we taught, for what is written in this book has been the fruit of experience that I taught them. Finally, thanks to rest of our family for their patience and support during the long hours of writing this book and above all there is the one almighty whose humble children we are. It is his blessings we cherish and pray for. It is the blessing we wish for you.

My special acknowledgment to all the authors whose books, journals and paper are referred while writing this book.

We deeply express my heartful thanks to the Management Team and Editorial Staff of Khanna Book Publishing Co. (P) Ltd. for printing the book in such a beautiful get-up and well in time.

When you finish the journey through this book, having variety of experiences, ideas, and thoughts. You are welcome to express your opinion at **contact@khannabooks.com.**

Author

CONTENTS

PART ONE

Fundamentals

1 Blockchain Technology & Bitcoin Beginnings

Before going into the details of working principles and other aspects of blockchain, let's look into the gensis of the technology itself. The conceptual framework behind blockchain was first put forward by a group of researchers in 1991. The idea was initially intended for time-stamping digital documents such that backdating them will not be possible thereafter. However, the idea went mostly unused until it was again mentioned by Satoshi Nakamoto in his white paper.

It may be the first time in history that the inventor of a game-changing technology has completely gone anonymous. Satoshi Nakamoto; an anonymous person/group is said to be behind the first blockchain came into existence and it was in 2009. In the following years, the bitcoin became popular, and the underlying technology became even more popular. So the confusion and lack of clarity among people start from the origin itself; a product and its related terminologies went viral before the technology behind it. And when the blockchain displayed its real potential, people were trying to relate it with bitcoin terminologies; the result was total misconception and confusion. But it is the other way; start from blockchain and then try to understand bitcoin. Blockchain is the underlying technology that many cryptocurrencies–like Bitcoin and Ethereum-operate on, but its unique way of securely recording and transferring information has broader applications outside of cryptocurency. A blockchain is a type of distributed ledge.

Blockchain has the potential to grow to be a bedrock of the worldwide record-keeping systems, but was launched just 10 years ago.

The advances in science and technology has gone to the new levels. The process in computational technology and ubiquitous computing is expanding exponentially day by day. People and services are moving towards clouds and decentralized platforms. The computer systems which was invented as a mere punching machines became an integral part of our lives. The size of the devices are getting smaller and faster. In today's world the mobile devices are on verge of replacing the desktop and handheld computers. Everything is being done on mobile phones. It is interesting to note that every decade gave us a revolution. Openness is the new mantra of today's world. The successful businesses in the world today are free. Companies like Facebook, Google, Twitter are propelling the world economy into the new direction.

1970's was the era of Mainframe computers, 1980's was the age when first PC was introduced, In the next decade of 1990's internet changed the world completely. It replaced the physical letters with email. Libraries and physical books with electronic books and portable documents. Internet has touched the like never before. In 2000's with the advent of mobile computing the size of the devices started to shrink. Telecommunication networks was the thing after the computing networks. Mobile phones has changed the world completely with new innovations. Now in the present decade the biggest revolution was created by an unknown computer genius, cryptography expert and a computer scientist who selflessly worked for several years in a community to provide the biggest gift to mankind. An instrument which is changing the economy of the world.

As the devices became smaller and smaller the software revolution substantiate it with the open source technologies, P2P sharing, Torrents and other platforms on lines of the Cypherpunk Movement.

The history of Blockchain and Bitcoin technology is also associated closely with the Financial crisis of 2009. Satoshi Nakamoto is considered as the father of Blockchain and Bitcoin technology. Satoshi was active on internet during the development phase of the technology. The last email communication with him was recorded on December 12th 2010 where in he sent a mail to Gavin Andresen, Lead Core Developer of the Bitcoin project after which he became inactive. Satoshi started working on the concept of a decentralized currency during the financial crisis of 2008 and registered a domain name *www.bitcoin.org* in August 2008. In October 2008 he published a white paper "Bitcoin : A peer to peer Electronic cash system which he announced on 1st November 2008 in a cryptography mailing list. The research paper which was published can be read in the Appendix section of this book. In January 2009, he published the source code of Bitcoin and Blockchain technology.

At the beginning of 2009 a genesis block was created, the genesis block is the first block in a complete block chain. We will understand genesis block in the later chapters of this book. In 2009 the first transaction of bitcoin happened using the blockchain technology. It is interesting to note that the blockchain technology is the super structure on which bitcoin is based. In May 2010 a real bitcoin transaction took place in which a man brought a pizza paying 10,000 bitcoins!! Considering the current value of the bitcoin, that is around 575 crore rupees for a single pizza isn't it the worlds most expensive pizza?

After few months in July 2010 the first bitcoin exchange was setup which was named "Mt.Gox". In February 2011, bitcoin became the world's first digital currency to exchange parity with the United States Dollar. From February 2011 to June 2012 Block Number 181919 became the largest block with 1322 transactions on a single blockchain. Don't worry if you are not able to connect with these terms as we will be going through all these in the coming chapters of this book.

But as the cryptocurrency became more and more popular people started to find more avenues of spending, acquiring, and trading it in the world market. Another benefit of this cryptocurrency was its anonymity. No one can trace the origin and destination of the receiver and sender. Therefore one dark web revolution happened with launch of "*Silk Route Marketplace*". Silkroute is a website which was inaugurated on darkweb, its a portal like ebay where users can buy and trade drugs and other illegal stuff which they cannot get easily in open world.

Bitcoin popularity and price rise also gave invitation to hackers all over the world to steal and hack bitcoins. The only biggest exchange "Mt.Gox was hacked and shut down by the group of hackers in 2012 when it went down for seven days with approximate loss of several thousand dollars. Soon governments around the world sensed bitcoin as a threat to their fiat currency[1] system and stated that this currency is harmful for the world economic order. In 2013 US government had a press release which stated that this kind of cryptocurrency will increase the terrorism in the world.

In June 2013, coin base a startup company for bitcoin wallet's raised 5 million US Dollars as a startup capital and also opened a first ATM machine in the state of San Diego US. This was for the first time the bitcoin price raised to 1,000$ which seemed as an exponential growth by many countries. In February 2014 "Mt.Gox" exchange was attacked again severely by hackers and was destroyed completely. Consequently it was shut down for ever. In 2014, Pay Pal the biggest online money exchanger and transaction carrier announced the bitcoin integration.

From year 2014 to 2018 many cryptocurrencies were launched and the price of bitcoin raised from mere Dollars 3000 to 537,000 Rupees per bitcoin and bitcoin price is still rising. New bitcoin exchanges are coming up everyday and bitcoin today has become the world's biggest cryptocurrency in world economy.

Satoshi Nakamoto became a household name and many journalist's and researchers tried to trace the man behind the blockchain and bitcoin technology without any luck. Recently a US newspaper identified a California engineer, Dorian Satoshi Nakamoto as the founder of blockchain technology but he himself denied any connection with bitcoin or cryptocurrency. Just

1 Flat currency: The legal currency of any counting used by government for its economy.

after the publication of the report in the paper. In March 2014 original Satoshi Namakato came online once again on the www.p2pfoundation.com forum and clarified that he is not Dorian Nakamoto.

In this way the technology and currency created and invented by an unknown identity sparked a new technological & economic revolution which is changing the world like never before. In the coming chapters of this book we will discuss the technology behind blockchain and cryptocurrencies in detail.

Many of the technologies we now take for granted were quite revolutions in their time. Just think how much smartphones have changed the way we time and work. It used to be that when people wee out of the office, they were gone, because a telephone was tied to a place, not a person. Now we have global nomads building new businesses straight from their phones. And to think, Smartphones have been around for merely a decade. Blockchain promises to solve this problem. The technology at the heart of bitcoin and other virtual currencies, blockchain is an open, distributed ledger that can record transactions between two parties efficiently and in a verifiable and permanent way. The ledger itself can also be programmed to trigger transactions automatically.

Blockchain technology made its public debut in Jan 2009 with Bitcoin, providing means for a decentralized, borderless, permissionless and trustless exchange of value without any bank or a central intermediary. Blockchain has disrupted currency, and is now disrupting various industries by bringing in a new form of '*digital trust*'. Blockchain is the new form of internet 2.0 and money 2.0!

2
Working of Conventional Money Market & Why do we need the Concept of Blockchain & Cryptocurrency

From a business perspective, it's helpful to think of blockchain technology as a type of next-generaion business process improvement software. Collaborative technology, such as blockchain, promises the ability to improve the business processes that occur between companies, radically lowering the "*cost of trust*". For this reason, it may offer significantly higher returns for each investment dollar spent than most traditional internal investments. Financial institutions are exploring how they could also use blockchain technology to upend everything from clearing and settlement to insurance.

For an overview of cryptocurency, start with money is no object. We explore the early days of bitcoin and provide survey data on consumer familiarity, usage and more. We also look at how market participants such as investors, technology providers, and financial institutions, will be affected as the market matures.

For an overview of blockchain in financial services, we examine same of the ways financial services firms are using blockchain, and how we expect the blockchain technology to develop in future. Blockchain is not a cure-all, but there are clearly many problems for which this technology is the ideal solution.

Let's remember an old civilization for a while, when there was no money. All the goods and services were bartered in the society. The producer of the milk shares and exchanges his produce with the farmers for grains. It was a simple society. The whole community was divided on the basis of the professions in which people are engaged. With the discover of copper the world moved into the copper age and finally a need for a common medium of exchange was realized and for the first time metal coins were used in China. Then after gold and silver coins were minted and they became prominent currency. Initially the value of these coins was based on the weight of the coin. It is also interesting to note that in almost every civilization of the world some kind of precious material copper, gold or silver was used to mint the primitive coins.

As the world became more organized and the forms of governments evolved, it called for new economic reforms. Government around the world started to use the paper money as the currency and decided to give away the phase use of precious metal for minting money. They started using non precious metals to mint coins. Government across the world took their gold reserve as a reference and started to print 70 - 80% equivalent money value and that money is circulated in the market. This is when the concept of the Fiat money came into picture. A fiat money is the money or the form of currency which was legalized by the government, without it its trash. Lets take the Indian context. The old 500 rupees and 1000 rupees notes are trash today. And a newly printed 2000 rupees notes has got a value. So the concept of fiat money is that the actual piece of coin or note does not have its intrinsic value unless it is backed by the government.

You must have also observed it that on Bank notes the RBI or the Reserve Bank of India promises the bearer the amount which he holds in his hand.

So, the government backed bond papers, your fixed deposits, *etc.* are kind of fiat currency being circulated in the market.

Government in this way take reference of its gold reserves and also considers other factors while printing money. For now you just need to understand that when a new currency is printed and introduced in the market people start to trade. Trade means any transaction involving money. Usually the new currency is circulated by government by using the banking system where all banks are directed to distribute new currencies. And here is when the banking system came into picture which is another important instrument of the economy.

Banks became a mediator and takes commission for transaction. They also use your money kept in your bank accounts for expanding their business and for that they pay you interest. They also act as a money lender, also facilitate the transfer of money from one place to another, one account to another and also act as an authority to issue bonds, fixed deposits and other investment instruments.

These banking system are strictly controlled by the government and central banks and they also control the inflation and deflation with the help of Repo and Reverse repo rates, banking rates and other monetary policies. If it sound's complicated then don't worry let's try to understand it with an interesting story.

Suppose you were walking on a sea shore and came across a blinking, glowing device. You approached it with uncertainty and curiosity and picked it up. The device had a green button and was like an alarm. Impulsively you pressed the button and moments later you arrived at a new planet in a galaxy which was barren and the planet was a primitive one. The people there were very poor and the world was like just evolved there recently. Those people were using the primitive stone tools and was a predominantly hunter and gatherer society.

Seeing you there with jeans and sports shoes with a mobile phone they were impressed and astonished (sounds wiered) and they enthroned you as the king of that planet and asked you to mange things there. Based on your own knowledge of earth you started building up their planet.

First thing you observed there was that they had no money so you asked them to find gold and silver and setup a mint factory. You asked them to measure the weight of the silver and gold coins. Here you are asking them to mint coins based on the weight of the metal as equivalent value.

The first distribution of the coins happened personally to the work force of the mint in form of their salaries. Then you overall distributed some currency to each citizen of your planet. After that you realized that those people are in need of some facilities like hospitals, schools, township, a colony, roads etc. You started the road construction first. So now as you have already distributed all your money and for building roads you need extra funds, you have two options.

1. Either you can actually collect the money in form of Taxes from the people for trading meat, grains, milk etc. But taxes can be implemented only to some extent as the world was primitive and there was not much trade happening there.
2. Second option is to borrow money from the people in form of bonds where you will promise them on a piece of paper that you will pay back their money at a certain time with some additional amount as interest.

Therefore you took money from the people but later on you realized that even this money is not sufficient for building hospitals and other infrastructure. Then you finally decide to make more coins.

You asked your team to dig out more silver, gold and copper but all reserves were empty.

Now as a leader you decided to call back every coin minted in your treasury and made a decision to shave these coins. Your employees shaved these coins metal and made those coins little smaller. After this exercise luckily your treasury was able to mint 50% more coins that you had initially in your system by using the shaved metal but when you introduced these coins in your markets, people realize that these coins were lighter than the previous coin and as their number increases in the market the value of each coin became less. This simple concept is called *Inflation*. Look how simple it is to understand with help of a metaphor.

Going by demand and supply also when more coins chase less goods value of the coin becomes less and things become more costly.

On other hand even if you have created addition coins by taking material from the existing circulated coins the amount of actual gold, copper and silver in the market was the same. And as the traders actually selling goods based on the weight of the coins, introducing new coins will not make any difference. As traders found these coins lighter the seller has to pay more number of coins to buy a product. (This is a simple concept of inflation where more coins chasing same goods but only theoretically). Practically there is no inflation and deflation in our scenario as the amount of precious metal chasing the goods was same even if new coins were minted by the shaved material. Remember we have our initial economy based on the weight of the coins in our story.

Now let's assume that you got frustrated that your problem was not solved. Therefore you decided to call back all currency. You asked your workers to melt copper, gold and silver in the furnace and directed them to create gold bricks. Then you issued some paper on which you wrote that this paper is worth 5 kg of gold and people wont believed you, you passed a law that this paper is actually worth 5 kg gold as a legal tender. This way you can actually attach any value to a thing like paper.

By using this instead of the metal, the law does its work and everything is in control. Here in this scenario you can actually control the inflation. Means by a law you can raise the value of money or you can decrease it by printing more notes as a legal tender. Inflation as an instrument is being used around the world to fulfill its promises to the people of the country. This system is closed and all people are in hands of the government for their money. The market value, exchange value and other parameters are decided by the government. This kind of arrangement is considered as an exploitative one by many. This is what happened in the Financial Crisis of 2008, which we will discuss in detail in the coming chapters.

Now lets say instead of solving your problem by using the paper legal tender which can be printed on demand. You fixed the amount of money in your world before hand. You declared that only 1000 units of money will be there in our world. So you printed 1000 notes. These notes were distributed to everyone in your world fairly. Now brainstorm the possibilities about this new economic system with fixed amount of currency.

In this case there will be no central authority that is controlling your money, there will no loss of value of money or inflation as no one can print more money and there will be a just system of economy based on demand and supply mechanism. In this scenario the value will be purely decided by the demand and supply. And this is what blockchain based cryptocurrencies does, they provide a decentralized economic order for the world.

Now let us answer a simple question. Why do we need Blockchain?

In a conventional money transfer process to your friend in United States requires you to fill form at your local bank account foreign exchange or remittances counter and then a request is generated for the payment. You need to provide your friends check in account and other details and after the confirmation the actual transaction actual funds will be received by your friend in his account after three days of initiating this transfer request. It also requires you to pay a substantial amount as the transaction fee to the bank. In this scenario your Indian bank acts as the trusted third party between you and your friend. The transaction fee levied by your bank depends on the amount being sended overseas *i.e.*, more the amount more will be the transaction fees.

Cost and Time makes these kinds of transactions inviable. This kind of transaction system is not viable in case of emergencies and urgent scenarios. This is why people generally take hawala route to send money across the globe.

This blockchain technology actually solves these kinds of business problems. Instead of sending money by using the banks route you buy a cryptocurrency token from a website and transfer it to your friend in US. Your friend can get this tokens in his wallet immediately and he can change them to his local currency (dollars in this case) anywhere in the market.

Therefore using blockchain for developing a cryptocurrency can solve this problem among others. Blockchain technology can help users to create a kind of self sustained and automated applications that can change the course of humanity. So we can safely say that this blockchain can help us to develop an equal economic system of the world and a solution for a new world order for the planet you landed accidentally! The evolution of this blockchain is very interesting which we will be taking up in the next chapter.

Blockchain announcements continue to occur, although they are less frequent and happen with less fanfare than they did a few years ago. Still, blockchain technology has the potential to result in a radically different competitive future for the financial services industry.

Blockchain increases trust, security, transparency, and the traceability of data shared across a business network and delivers cost savings with new efficiencies. Blockchain for business uses a shared and immutable ledger that can only be accessed by members with permissions.

3

Evolution: Cryptography, Cypherpunk

The crypto industry tends to give "Cypherpunk" vibes a great deal of lip service without much attention to their real values. Back in 1990s, prescient software guys got both excite about the internet and anxious about a future in which it would ruin every meaningful bit of privacy.

A cypherpunk is an individual advocating widespread use of strong cryptography and privacy–enhancing technologies as a route to social and political change. Originally communicating through the cypherpunks electronic mailing list, informal groups aimed to achieve privacy an security through proactive use of cryptography. Cypherpunks have been engaged is an active movement since at least the lae 1980s.

Until about the 1970s, cryptography was mainly practiced in secret by military or spy agencies. However, that changed when two publications brought it into public awareness; the US government publication of Data Encryption Standard (DES), a block cipher which became very widely used; and the first publicly available work or public – key cryptography, by Whitfield Diffie and Martin Hellman.

The technical roots of cypherpunk ideas have been traced back to work by cryptographer David Chaum on topics such as anonymous digital cash and pseudonymous reputation systems, described in his paper "*Security without Identification: Transaction Systems to Make Big Brother Obsolete*" (1985).

The earliest form of cryptography was a cipher (a cipher is an algorithm used for encryption or decryption). Ciphers had the problem of being easily broken using the frequency of the letters, and once a generalized way of breaking them was found they became obsolete. The first known evidence of cryptography can be traced to the se of '*hieroglyph*'. Some 4000 years ago, the Egyptians used to communicate by messages written in hieroglyph. This code was the secret known only to the scribes who used to transmit messages on behalf of the kings.

Technologies are not created in a single day. Lot of ground work have to be done by various computer scientist and programmers for decades to bring a concept to reality. They say that necessity is the mother of all inventions and here a need of cryptocurrency led to the invention of blockchain technology.

Therefore, it is important to understand the historical perspective the motivations behind the evolution of this system. Theoretically there are four major components that has immensely contributed to the evolution of blockchain as a technology. "Cyberpunk Movement", Financial Crisis of 2008 provided the ethical foundations for the technology to evolve. The technical concepts of cryptography, distributed system provides the solid technical foundations.

There is a specific branch of computer science and mathematics known as cryptography which has made the evolution of this blockchain technology possible. Cryptography is nothing but a process of concealing information from all and providing access to only the person to whom the information is addressed to. Only the intended receiver can access and read the information. Initially cryptography was used only by American and European spying agencies & military for Secret communication. But after 1970 Dr Whitfield Diffue and Dr Martin Hell Man changed the world and made cryptography accessible to the common world. They published a paper titled "New Directions in cryptography" which was followed by the publication of the data encryption standard by the United States Government. Dr David Chaum presented the idea of anonymous digital cash pseudo repetition systems in his paper "*Security without identification transaction systems to make a big brother obsolete*" in early 90's. These widespread ideas in the scholarly community work propagated for several years and took a shape of a movement in 1990. In 1992. Timothy C May, Eric Huges and John Gilmore formed a small group cypherpunk from the word cypher and punk. A mailing list was formed and they started to write and mail papers. One such paper titled "*Cypherpunks Manifesto*" for the first time talked about the concept of privacy in their own words. They wrote privacy is necessary for an open security in the electronic age. A privacy is not secrecy. Private matter is something one doesn't want the whole world to know but a secret matter is something one doesn't want anybody to know privacy is the power to selectively reveal oneself to the world.

Some prominent members who were and still are part of the cypherpunk movement include the greatest whistle blower and founder of WikiLeaks Julian Assange; the top developer Jacob Appelbaum the creator of bittorrent client and bittorrent Technology.

In late 1990, in the cyber world so many crypto wars were fought that the time when government wanted to push back the movement and they were fighting to supress an individual's privacy. In the end the government lost that war and privacy and also piracy became an integral part of the world.

In 1998 the philosophical foundation of cryptocurrency can be seen in a paper by Wei Die who published the proposal for money which was a contractual agreement between autonomous parties for sending and receiving money.

In 2005 Nik Sabzo published proposal for bit gold which was a sort of currency purely based on reusable proof of work for concept but in 2008 Satoshi Nakamoto which is a pseudo name and we don't know is 1 or a group of people published a bitcoin whitepaper and in this white paper he has cited the works of scientist who worked on the concept of Hash cash and B money.

Satoshi also mentioned that he has learned about the Bhim money from Dr Adam Back. Satoshi himself has written about privacy in his own published white paper.

He said the traditional banking model achieves a level of privacy by limiting access to information to the parties involved the trusted third party. The necessity to announce all transactions publicly precludes this method can still be maintained by breaking the flow of information in another place. By keeping public key anonymous the public can see that someone is sending an amount to someone else but make clearer without information linking the transaction to anyone this is similar to the level of information released by stock exchanges where the time and size of the individual trades the tape is made public but without telling who the parties were.

So in this way cypherpunk movement somehow became the motivation and need for the new technology and the financial crisis of 2008 which have trickle down effects on the world economy. Computer scientists and cryptographers across the world tried two revolutionaries the world economic system by introducing blockchain based decentralized and distributed electronic currency has contributed to the development of blockchain technology to work on the solution for world economy.

4

Financial Crisis of 2008

Following the 2008 global financial crisis, the world's first digital cryptocurrency (Bitcoin) was proposed. The introduced platform allowed peer-to-peer (P2P) transactions to take place, eliminating the need for intermediary financial authorities, being the first fully decentralized commercial system of its kind. The aggressive rising of interest rates is commonly viewed as a leading recession indicator. Following the news, the stock market as well the crypto market witnessed a huge downfall, investors lost trust and started selling off their digital assets, causing a bloodbath in the crypto market.

Cryptocurrency trading throws around alleged millions and billions. Those numbers are fictions built on fictions, with a much smaller but still real – amount of actual money at the bottom. The gateways to genuine dollars are narrow and have yet to be significantly breached. But that's not for lack of effort from the cryptocurrency world, whose endgame appears to be to make cryptocurrency systematic and leave the government as the bag-holder of last resort when the tottering heaps of leverage fall down. It worked in 2008, after all.

Cryptocurrency started in 2009 with idealistic dreams of a new economy built on libertarian principles and freedom from the fiat currency system that had just crashed. But in 2002, cryptocurrency trading is all about the dollars and the 2008 financial crisis has just repeated in absurd miniature.

In the previous chapter we have discussed the two psychological motivations associated with the invention of blockchain technology. The third one is the impact of the financial crisis as the motivation. Blockchain and Bitcoin were announced after the financial crisis of 2008 and it was an important event because Satoshi made remarks about this in his white papers. Therefore its imperative to understand the crisis which had a deep impact on the world economy.

The prices of housing and real estate across the world was rising. Just after the Second World war (1945), world economy was gaining momentum and property was considered as a safe avenue to park funds. Real estate markets became quite lucrative for the people to invest. People from all classes, irrespective of their financial backgrounds started investing in the property. White collar workers took the advantage of easy lending schemes from the banks heavily for their investments.

Specially in the United States market in 1980's big financial organizations realized that the US mortgage markets have potential for making money and are unexplored. Traders at the prominent financial institutions. Salomon Brothers and Drexel Burnham Lambert decided to expand this bond market operations.

They reorganized the structure of the bond market and observed a steady stream of payments from the home owners across the United States. This means that all the people who took Home Loans are paying their loan installments on time because of the good wages earned by the white collar lenders.

Soon the banks also realized this and they themselves mortgages can be restructured as the bonds and can be sold to the big institutions as an financial instrument, *i.e.* bonds backed by the mortgages.

It happened by chance that the US government reduced the federal bank rate. This is the rate at which banks can lend money.

In May of year 2000 the rate was 6.5% which came down to mere 1.75% in 2001 which was a drastic 75% decrease in one year! Further in 2003 the rate touched to record 45 years low of 1%. This decrease has encouraged thousands of investors and home seekers to take more home loans from the financial institutions. This meager rate of 1% also encouraged people from low income group to seek loans for their houses.

Another factor that millions of people jumped in was because real estate investments were considered as a good investment and all the investors and home owners were optimistic that sooner the real estate prices will rise and sooner they will sell their house and they will came out from the mortgage after making some good profits. But at the same time majority of the loans went to the people who were not capable to repay their loans.

Slowly the Interest rare started to rise again in 2007 -2008. The borrowers had taken the loan in form of adjustable rates (Floating Lending Ratesin Indian Economy). When there was a rise in the interest rates borrowers were not able to repay. Finally the lenders defaulted on their loans.

But as we have seen that those loans were already sold to the big corporations as an investment instruments backed by the mortgage. When lenders defaulted and surrendered their loans their properties were confiscated and buyers of the bonds filed bankruptcy. During this period many mammoth financial institutions went down. One of our common friend came back from US during this period because he lost his job. Overall there was a loss of approximately one trillion dollars.

Governments tried their best to improve the situation by decreasing the lending rates and adjusting the rate of interest at the lower levels but eventually the US financial markets crashed and it had a trickle down effect on the world economy.

This situation, according to Satoshi called for a new decentralized, distribution and self equilibrating economic system and the rise of bitcoin & blockchain happened after this crisis. Therefore in a way this financial crisis provided a sort of motivation to find out a new alternative economic system in form of cryptocurrency and blockchain together as a package.

5
Computer System Architecture

Today everyone has realized that a single isolated computer kept in a room is only capable of performing selected operations. Everyone is connected with each other on Internet. You can place order, communicate and can share files by using this super network. The world is on your fingertips.

When Internet was started in 1998 it was developed initially for the military communication, but sooner it became widespread enough to touch humanity alike.

The way computers are connected with each other is very interesting. A computer at your home can be connected by wireless network with your broadband modem provided by MTNL, Airtel or BSNL. When your computer is connected to the Internet, theoretically you are connected to all other computer in the world which are also connected to the Internet. Although your computer is connected with every other connected on Internet but, both can only communicate for specific services because they are behind a firewall and have only specific opened ports. For example for accessing Internet port number 80 is required, for FTP port number 23 needs to be opened.

Ports are like the sea shore trade ports in a country when any commercial ship loaded with the consignment comes to the port it is anchored at the destination country's ports and then initiate a business transaction after a proper paper work. Only after a proper authentication and custom clearance the goods are unloaded in the destination country.

In similar manner these ports in the computer system are used to provide services of receiving and sending authenticated data from source computer to the destination computer on the network.

When you type in yahoo.com and a page is displayed on your web browser that page is actually residing in another computer at a different location (server). Your computer requests the other computer and this transaction or data exchange happens on Port 80 usually. Irrespective of the distance that computer serves your request by displaying Yahoo's Home page on your computer.

But its only a macro view of a computer transaction in reality there are many technicalities involved which are not required for you to understand the concept of functioning of cryptocurrencies.

This client server architecture holds true for over internet (as in yahoo's example) as well as for the locally connected computers. When you use your office's print server for taking print out's or accessing a document located on your office file server are two scenarios where client server architecture is present on local network.

Now lets move a little bit further to define "*Computer System Architecture*".

Centralized System

In computer science the Computer System Architecture is a concept which explains how systems are connected with each other either locally or over Internet. It is also possible to have multiple servers and clients in a network. But when there is a single server catering to the needs of multiple computers then in this scenario only one server is providing services to number of client computers & in this case we can say that it's a centralized system. Centralized means a central authority or a central system is serving multiple clients. So in case if the central system have some problem then that system will not able to serve his clients and the services will be affected. But these kind of system has an advantage also they are very easy to manage and they are simple systems so one can update or modify change according to personal requirements very easily.

Decentralized System

Decentralized system is a kind of arrangement where there is more than one sever catering to the need of various clients. For example if there are four servers in a network where in each server is serving four clients and servers themselves are connected with each other then its a decentralized system.

The main benefit of a decentralized system is that it helps in load sharing as the amount of work is now shared among four servers. Another important aspect is that in case of any problem in one server still other clients can work having less impact on business operations.

Distributed System

In this kind of arrangement the components of various computers are located across the distant geographic area and often communicate with each other to achieve a common goal. These systems can work as a server or a client on the basis of received requests. Most of the cryptocurrency networks are based on this kind of computing paradigm.

Each of the explained set of systems has advantages and disadvantages. centralized systems are easy to maintain as there is only a single point of failure. Decentralized have more but still finite. Distributed systems are the most difficult to maintain but they can be maintained with help of computing algorithms like in case of Blockchain networks.

The thumb rule of selecting the paradigm is that If there is a strong sever capable of serving all users then one should go for a centralized system. But if there are multiple servers and administrators to manage each server then one should go for a decentralized setup. But if there are number of computers participating in the network as contributors a distributes kind of system makes more sense.

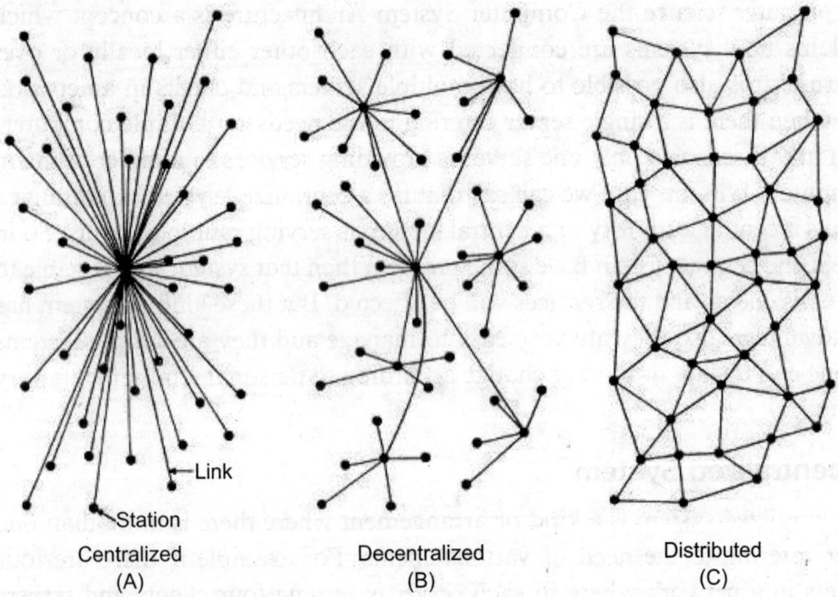

A - Centralized System

B - Decentralized System

C - Distributed System

This decentralized distributed computing architecture plays a very important role in the functioning of blockchain. The concept is that anyone can modify it after authentication and can share their computing power for work in return for some tokens.

6
Forking & Open Source Technology

Forking is to take the source code from an open source software program and develop an entirely new program. Forking is often the result of a deadlock in an open source project that is so insurmountable that all work stops.

Free and Open-Source Software is that which, by definition, may be forked from the original development team without prior permission and without vidating copyright law. However, licensed forks of proprietary software (e.g. Unix) also happen.

In software engineering, a project fork happens when developers take a copy of source code from one software package and start independent development on it, creating a distinct and separate piece of software. The term often implies not merely a development branch, but also a split in the developer community as such, it is a form of schism. Grounds for forking are varying user preferences and stagnated or discontinued development of the original software.

In proprietary software, the copyright is usually held by the employing entity, not by the individual software developers. Proprietary code is thus more commonly forked when the owner needs to develop two or more versions such as a windowed version and a command line version, or versions for different operating systems, such as a word processor for IBM PC compatible machines and Macintosh Computers. Generally, such internal forks will concentrate on having the same look, feel, data format, and behaviour between platforms so that a user familiar with one can also be productive or share documents generated on the other. This is almost always an economic decision to generate a greater market share and thus pay back the associated extra development costs created by the fork. A notable proprietary fork not of this kind is the many varieties of proprietary Unix–almost all derived from AT & T Unix under license and all called "Unix", but increasing mutually incompatible.

Before we dive into the Blockchain and Bitcoin sections of this book let's understand few technical concepts. These concepts are simple yet important from functional point of view. You may also encounter these terms regularly on Internet. These terms which we are going to understand are connected to the world of blockchain and as a software domain as a whole. First concept is "Open Source Technologies". You might have Windows or Mac system running in your desktop or laptop computer. During its purchase the operating system was provided by your computer hardware manufacturer. This means that Windows or Mac software was pre installed in your computer since the day one. In this scenario the cost of this operating system either Windows or Mac OS was added to the cost of the hardware by your computer supplier. So you haven't paid for the operating system separately. Another important feature of these operating systems is that they don't share the source code to anyone and their source code is confidential. Sharing of source code means that only specific people in the company can make changes in Windows & Mac OS functionality.

But have you heard of any free operating system? The one which you can use freely. There are the chances that you have heard of " Linux" or "Unix" operating system. This "Linux" & "Unix" operating systems are free to use and can be easily downloaded from Internet. They are also free to modify and open source is also available to all. So in general we can say that there are two kinds of operating systems, Windows or Mac OS where you need to pay licensing fees to Microsoft and Apple and they have restricted code. These companies invest money to hire people, resources and research for launching new improved version of Windows and Mac OS after certain intervals.

The second type "Linux" & "Unix" are the free ones, their research and development is done by the voluntary developers who want to contribute to the free software and they are open code softwares. Many a times they are also adopted and funded by other commercial companies but still they keep it as free and code is also made available for all to download.

A similar kind of rules applies for all the software domain. Here software domain means any kind of software whether its an operating system or a word processor or any kind of software. In open source software there are many specific licenses and guidelines by which anyone can launch a new software on the basis of existing software. These separate license types is out of scope of this book but one of the most popular license in open source is the GNU license which is also called as *General Public License*.

So, Bitcoin and Blockchain are the open source software which was launched and source code was uploaded for everyone by its founder Satoshi Namakato. The largest repository on Internet for open source software is *www.sourceforge.net* where you can download free software with a modifiable source code for your various needs without paying a single penny! But what if some changes needs to be made in the existing software according to your own business or personal requirement?

Then there are two possibilities:

First, you do a minor modification like adding a field or changing a name of a field or adding a new button etc. In this case the modification is minor and therefore its called a soft fork version of the software (Soft forking of a software).

Second, but lets assume for a moment that you have downloaded the software and the source code but your business requirement is such that you have hired a team of developers and you need to change the core components of the software according to your own business requirement. In this case it hardly matters that you are hiring a team or you are asking a single competent person to modify its code but here the core components of the existing software needs to be changed and therefore this modification is called as Hard Fork and process is hard forking. Usually hard fork softwares are not backward compatible.

These soft forks and hard forks has been used continuously in the block chains and cryptocurrencies to make them scalable and also to launch new versions of cryptocurrencies. If you remember in previous chapters we have discussed that the Satoshi Nakamoto published the original code on *sourceforge.net* which was used by others to modify and launch their own cryptocurrencies.

In this way these technologies are used regularly to generate new breed of cryptocurrencies, we will discuss some important forking's and how new currencies emerged because of this process in the coming chapters of this book.

PART TWO
Blockchain

7
Blockchain Introduction

Blockchain is the backbone technology of digital cryptocurrency bitcoin. The blockchain is a distributed database of records of all transactions or digital event that have been executed and shared among participating parties. Each transaction verified by the majority of participants of the system. It contains every single record of each transaction. Bitcoin is the most popular cryptocurrency an example of the blockchain. Blockchain technology records transaction in digital ledger which is distributed over the network thus making it incorruptible. Anything of value like land assets, cars, etc. can be recorded on blockchain as a transaction.

One key difference between a typical database and a blockchain is how the data is structured. A blockchain collects information together in groups, known as blocks, that hold sets of information. Blocks have certain storage capacities and, when filled, are closed and linked to the previously filled block, forming a chain of data known as the blockchain. All new information that follows that freshly added block is compiled into a newly formed block that will then also be added to the chain once filled.

A database usually structures its data into tables, whereas a blockchain, as its name implies, structures its data into chunks (blocks) that are strung together. This data structure inherently makes an irreversible timeline of data when implemented in a decenralized nature. When a block is filled, it is set in stone and becomes a part of this timeline Each block in the chain is given an exact timestamp when it is added to the chain.

As we have touched upon the fact that blockchain is the technology behind all the popular cryptocurrencies especially bitcoin. Blockchain was used by a group of researchers in 1991 to time stamp the documents. But again it was revived by Satoshi in 2009. This code of blockchain was initially embedded in the bitcoin currency as it was first used as the part of cryptocurrency programming. Blockchain is a kind of technology which can be used to develop different kind of applications as well. Use of blockchain for programming cryptocurrencies like bitcoin is only one of its application. In the previous section we have discussed the scenario when bank act as a mediator or transferring money from one country to other. In similar way blockchain as a system act as an autonomous mediator when its used for implementing cryptocurrency. It also handles all kind of disputes, validates and is capable of authenticating transactions and rewarding successful participants with help of mathematical functions and algorithms. Therefore blockchain actually provides bank or government level trust without a single government like entity. Every day new applications are coming up by using blockchain as a super structure but currently its use in cryptocurrencies is very prominent. Literally blockchain can be used to program any application based on the business requirement. It can be used for managing digital documents, equity or any other physical or digital asset. Now Lets understand what actually is a blockchain with an example. Have you ever saw red ledger books being kept by the whole sale market business men usually in shelves of their shops or on their desk during the business hours? A business man records all transactions including credit entries, debit entries, money coming going, inventory and stock information and other important details of his business. For him its like a bank pass book. Now image if there is a fire in his shop and his ledger were lost? What will happen?

His whole business will come down to ashes because the single important thing essential for his business was the ledger which had all the records of the transaction is lost. The business man will not able to know about his money lenders, receivable payments and about the money he need to pay to his suppliers. He will also be unaware of the price at which he has sold specific goods to certain set of traders. But what if man was smart enough and he had photocopies of this leisure kept at various places in delhi say one copy at his friends house, one at his in laws house and one at his own home. In this case the probability of loosing ledger from all locations at the same time is next to impossible compared to a single copy at his own workplace.

The blockchain is like the red ledger of that businessman which has all transaction information. In computer language we call it a database. A database is a big file which has records. The contact and phone number in your mobile phone is a database, your passbook entry for last one year is a database. A database is a set of information stored in a file at a place either in a computer or in physical form.

Blockchain is a kind of an intelligent autonomous database, this database records every completed transaction & shows it up chronologically on the top position. When you join any cryptocurrency network (Bitcoin) then you will get a unique identification number like a bank account number after the sign up process. Right then a new block is assigned to you for recording your performed transactions. Based on the number of transactions carried out by you the data is populated in the block and also that is updated to the cryptocurrency network. Each block in a blockchain can have thousands of transaction information stored. Transparency is also maintained in case of a public blockchain because anyone can look at the transactions without knowing the identity of the sender or receiver. Anyone can access bitcoin blockchain visiting *www.blockchain.info* as it is an open blockchain.

This blockchain database at the same time is distributed in thousands of computers connected to the ***INTERNET*** in the world. Like the red ledger kept at your inlaws house! Lets try to make it little bit more simpler. Suppose the businessman took the red ledger and daily before checking out from his shop he inserted all the details of the transactions daily in one excel file in his computer. That excel file becomes the database of the business man. But if he is storing the entries in a file located on his own computer in his shop then this is called a centralized database because there is only one file and that too located on the businessman's own computer. Remember the concept of decentralized and centralized architecture from part one of this book.

The blockchain database works on the concept of decentralized computing where a blockchain is accessed, modified, deleted and updated by all participants who take participation in mining. Here the participants are the hundreds of computers connected with each other through internet in a certain blockchain application. Mining is a process of adding new records in a blockchain and we will discuss this concept further in this book. A blockchain application can be classified as a *Public Blockchain* or *a Private Blockchain*. A private blockchain is a kind of chain where the participants are selected and have given access to the chain by its creator. In a private block chain, it is not possible for anyone to contribute and participate in the transactions and mining. This kind of blockchain can be used in private institutions for business purposes. The public blockchain is a blockchain which can be accessed by anyone and anyone can contribute to its chain and can participate in its mining. Therefore blockchain is a kind of a technology or a set of algorithms which handles all tasks of modifying, authenticating, maintaining a particular chain of records. This blockchain system also reward users and contributors for participating in the transactions.

Now you must be thinking that if this blockchain database is open for all to modify and access then how is it secure? This is a valid question. To answer this question you need to wait for few more chapters in this book but at this point you should understand that as blockchain database is decentralized and a single database is present in multiple computers across the globe, it is very difficult for a hacker to change all the existing copies in the world! If a blockchain is a bank account passbook and its copies are distributed among your trusted family members who resides in various countries and among all family members and every member is registered in your banking system and when ever you do a transaction he receives a debit or credit message on his mobile phone and after getting a ***SMS*** all family members are updating their copies and they are receiving some kind of rewards for this help and to ensure a fool proof system. Now if you have understood this scenario then this is a simplest example of a blockchain.

Lets discuss an another example. Let us assume there are three people Amit, Rahul and Gaurav. Amit gave 12 rupees to Rahul and Rahul gave 8 rupees to Gaurav so after these transaction we can conclude that Amit has 12 rupees less that what he had after giving it to Rahul and Rahul has 12 Rupees more than what he had after receiving it from Amit and in similar way Gaurav has now 8 rupees less than what he had after receiving it from Rahul. These types of transactions are entered in a block to form a chain of blocks also known as Blockchain and this is why is is also called as a Ledger. Once this blockchain database is distributed or copied in every participating computer then its really hard to tamper. Even if someone tries tampering the algorithm checks the local copy with the rest of the existing copies in the world and it deletes the tampered copy because the transaction or the database copy residing in multiple computers across the globe is deemed as the accurate or genuine copy.

In the conventional monetary system there are third party validators Paypal, Local Bank, Escrow which takes care of authentication and validations of a specific transactions. In blockchain technology this validation is taken care by the system by the process of mining. As discussed that after a successful validation of the transaction some reward is provided to the mining computer. Any computer in the world can join a blockchain mining network to help in transactions for some quick money. As these validations are carried out by solving complex mathematical problems, these are very secure and generally use hash functions. When a transaction is validated it is added to the blockchain database. Sometimes a single block has thousands of transaction records. In this way a blockchain is a never ending database of entries of the transactions providing solution for different business problems. We will be discussing some case studies in a separate chapter.

8
Blockchain Structure

A Genesis Block is the name given to the first block a cryptocurrency, such as Bitcoin, ever mined. A blockchain consists of a series of so - called blocks that are used to store information related to transactions that occur on a blockchain network. A block is composed of a header and a body, where a header contains the hash of previous block, a timestamp, nonce and the Merkle root.

The blockchain architecture consists of the elements like a node – user or computer that has a complete copy of the blockchain ledger, block - a data structure used for keeping a set of transactions, and transaction – the smallest building block of a blockchain system (records, information, etc.). All block in a specific order are arranged in a chain with miners that held to verify each block. The process inside the system is arranged according to a consensus protocol.

Blockchain is a P2P network where no single participant (user) controls the transaction the power is distributed among all the participants in this network, which means no single stakeholder can hack, manipulate or close the chain of blocks or can shut it down.

With the increasing number of blockchain systems appearing, even only those that support cryptocurrencies, blockchain interoperability is becoming topic of major importance. The objective is the support transferring assets from one blockchain system to another blockchain system. Wegner stated that "*interoperability is the ability of two or more software components to cooperate despite differences in language, interface, and execution platform*". The objective of blockchain interoperability is therefore to support such cooperation among blockchain ststems, despite those kinds of differences.

There are already several blockchain interoperability solutions available. They can be classified into three categories; cryptocurrency interoperability approaches, blockchain engines, and blockchain connectors.

Several individual IETF participants produced the draft of a blockchain interoperability architecture.

This chapter is little bit technical so readers are recommended to sit back with a cup of coffee and relax. In coming few pages we will try to understand the internal mechanism of blockchain working, so that you can dissect the technology which is behind the development of block and cryptocurrencies in general. A basic structure of a block has mainly four components. Starting with first is the:

1. Block Size which has the information of the size of the block.
2. Block Header contains the vital information about the identity of the block. Block header is an important part of the block structure and is further divided into various fields.
3. Transaction Counter this is a simple incremental counter of number of transaction in a particular block.
4. The last one is the Transaction.

In this all details of the transactions are present of the corresponding block (Fig. 8.1).

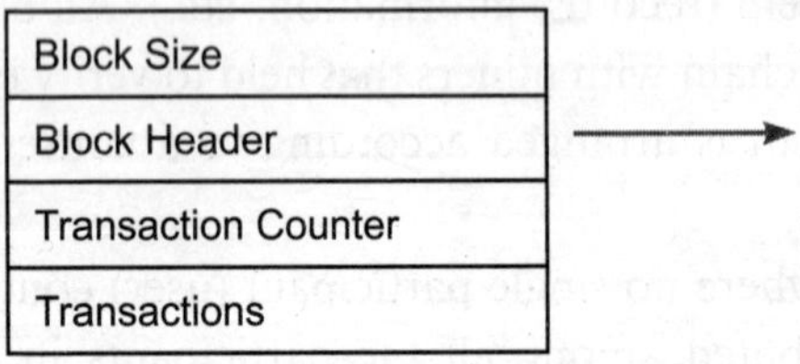

Fig. 8.1: *A Block Structure*

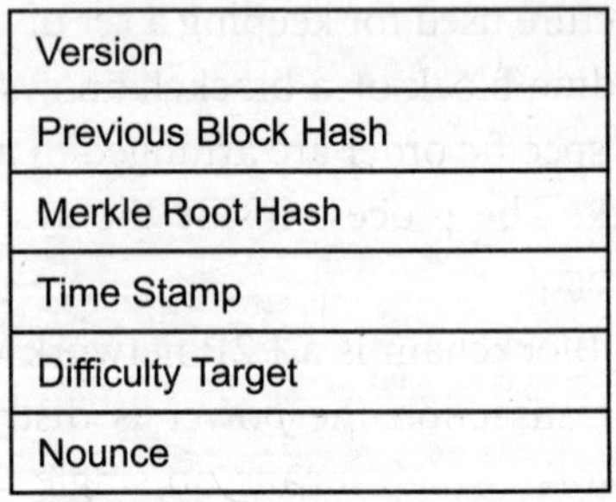

Fig. 8.2: *Fields of Block Header*

Now lets come back to the Block Header, which is an important field and contains lot of vital information about a particular block. The Header is divided into mainly six fields (Fig. 8.2).

1. Version field contains the protocol version of the blockchain.
2. Previous Block Hash its a hash of the entire previous block.
3. Merkle Root Hash, its the hash of the root of the Merkle Tree. All the transactions from the (Fig. 8.1) are processed by a merkle tree and then are inserted into the Merkle Root Hash field of the Block header. We will understand the functioning of the Merkle Tree later in this chapter. For now let us only understand that Merkle Root Hash is created with help of Merkle Tree.

4. Time stamp has the approximate creation of time and it uses the UNIX time function.
5. Difficulty target is a proof of work for the corresponding block.
6. At last we have a Nounce or a Random Number used for the proof of work algorithm.

Now lets understand how multiple blocks are joined and linked together to form a chain with help of a figure. Imagine in Fig. 8.1, three blocks Block A, B & C have a separate independent structure like this. There is not any maximum number of blocks because new blocks are added at every chain. With bitcoin, on average,every 10 minutes, a new block is added.

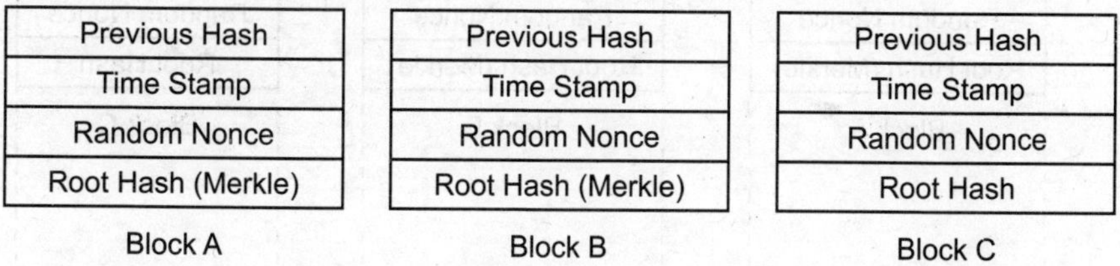

We have included only important fields of the block in the diagram for illustration. Previous Hash, Time Stamp, Random Nonce and Root Merkle or Root Hash. These four fields are used for the core functions of the block chain. In the following diagram T1, T2 & T3 are the transactions attached to Root Hashes of the three blocks as illustrated in Fig. 8.3.

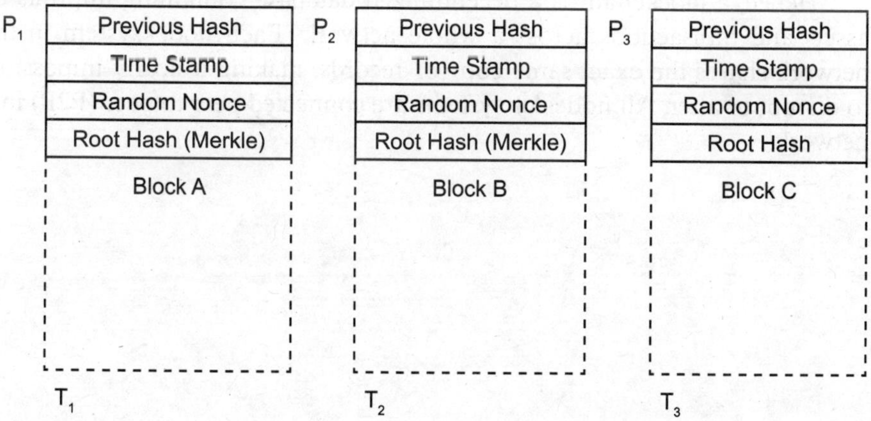

Fig. 8.3

As we have discussed in the last chapter that the first ever block in a blockchain is a Genesis Block. Here Block A can be considered as a genesis block because the structure of all blocks are same with only one difference in the previous Hash Value. It is blank in case of a Genesis Block. Rest of the values are automatically populated in the block by using the statistical methods. So we can say that the Block A previous value is blank because it is the first block in the block chain. Now lets see how the values of Block B will be generated by using the Genesis Block A's fields.

The Previous Hash Value of Block A is empty because its a Genesis Block. In a blockchain the entire Hash of the block becomes the value of the previous hash on the next block. Therefore in our figure. P2 value will be the value of the Hash of Block A & P3 will be generated as the Hash of Block B and so on. (As illustrated in the Fig. 8.4).

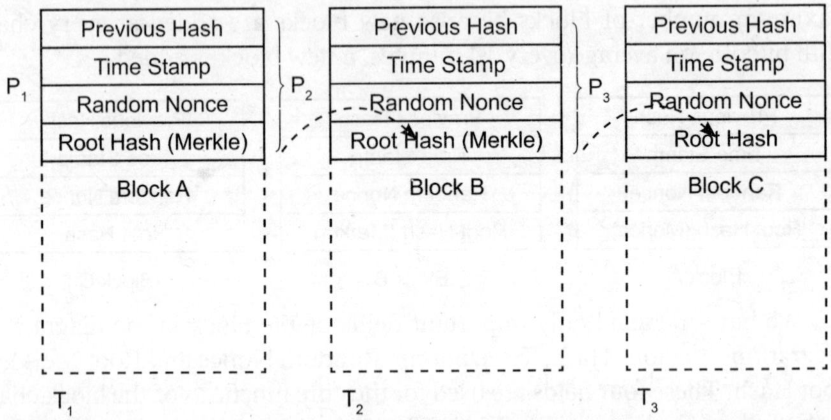

Fig. 8.4

Hence, a blockchain is a decentralized database containing imprints of assets and transactions across a whole network. Each node/system in the network shares the exact same copy of records, making it nearly impossible to disrupt or alter. All nodes or systems are connected peer to peer (P2P) in a network.

9

Core Concepts of Blockchain Cryptography, Hashing Function & Merkle Tree

Till now in this book we have discussed the functioning of blockchain technology and other introductory concepts. We have also seen blockchain as a foundation technology. Some of the most popular cryptocurrencies in the world are using blockchain technology as a super structure. Bitcoin, Ethereum, Litecoin and Ripple are some cryptocurrencies which are popular in today's world and gaining a fast momentum worldwide. But you must be wondering that how blockchain technology can facilitate the evolution of cryptocurrencies? As we have leaned in the previous chapters that concept of decentralization and distributed computing are the two pillars of the blockchain technology which helped blockchain technology to grow. The blockchain technology is not controlled by any single entity and is distributed over a large network which makes it fool proof. Another solid foundation of blockchain is the solid feature of accessibility to all, with hundred percent anonymity which is provided with the mathematical functions called as hashing in computational world. Hashing uses cryptography. All cryptographic concepts uses the substitution and transportation techniques to hide data.

In this chapter we will learn little bit of cryptography to understand how the information is hidden by using maths. Cryptocurrencies are the medium of exchanging digital tokens who number is usually fixed. 21 million coins in case of bitcoin. And this maximum value is fixed in the Genesis Block[1] while launching a specific cryptocurrency. In bitcoin's Genesis Block the value 21 million is unchanged and it will make sure that once all 21 million coins are generated the blockchain will stop creating new bitcoins. This limit in bitcoin makes it more interesting because of the demand and supply mechanism. Once all 21 million bitcoins are generated by the system and further production is stopped the coins are speculated to increase in its value due to market forces. It is believed that all bitcoin's will be exhausted by 2150 AD.

Coming back to the mathematical functions, the whole system of blockchain and it's application works on a complex algorithm's of cryptography. Cryptography in layman's term is an art of secret communication. Cryptography

1. The first block in a block chain

has been used by military since a long time to send encrypted messages during the war fare. Later on cryptography was used generally by public for personal privacy and securing communication. Today cryptography is quite complex. There are complex mathematical functions being used to encrypt and decrypt data. Suppose you want to send this message secretly to a friend.

"How Are you "

And you typed on a piece of paper "IPX0BSF0XPV"

This is the simples form of cryptography to understand encryption decryption and personal key. So when you sent him this letter, You called your friend or you met him probably (I know it sounds funny but we need to understand this!) and told him that when you receive my message you need to subtract one alphabet and also you have to replace "0" with a space.

So your friend received this message in his mailbox next day and he used your instructions to read "How Are You".

Here in this scenario the meaningless string "IPX0BSF0XPV" is your encrypted message. The instructions are your key and the received message after applying your instruction to the string by your friend is the decrypted message and the process of applying this key to the encrypted message is the decryption.

But as stated this is the simplest metaphor of cryptography one can imagine. But in actual practical applications in computing or those days warfares a complex method is devised by using mathematical functions. Lets say you will jumble up the message– "How Are You" by using the position of alphabet, squared its position and convert it to fraction of the adjacent numbers, then how complex the problem would be. The more complex the problem, chances of knowing your key or decrypting your messages become less. In today's world of computing very complex mathematical functions are used. In our case when we have squared the position of the number and calculating fractions of the next digits is a kind of mathematical function being used to encrypt message. These kinds of complex mathematical functions including prime numbers are used in process of cryptography. In day to day computer usage logging to any website including accessing your mails are using these kinds of cryptographic functions. The earliest known example of the cryptographic technique is the "*Caesar Cipher*".

In blockchain these functions are used extensively for security. The most important concept being used to make the blockchain reality is the concept of Hashing.

A hash function takes a variable sized input message and produces a fixed-sized output. The output is usually referred to as the hash code or the hash value or the message. This means that the information is encrypted in a block or values are processed in a set. For example, the SHA-512 Hash Function takes for input messages of length up to 2128 bits and produces as output a 512-bit message.

In a blockchain technology a Hashing Algorithms are used for securing the complete blockchain which is a type of cryptography. A hash is a one way function this means that the hashing algorithm will take some data as input and give out some random string of numbers as output. This is called one way function because it can not be reversed like in normal cryptographic function discussed earlier. So if you will get the random strings of numbers then you cannot get back to the original string. The hashing function of cryptography can be applied to any file. It can be used on a word file, on an image or any digital document. So hashing in the simples term is a function that takes some digital content and convert it into some numbers which is called as *Hash*. A very common format of Hashing is in the hexadecimal format.

Another important thing to note is that any slight modification in the input value can change the output completely, this includes any addition of space of change in a single number or alphabet of the input string.

If you are not able to understand this then don't worry here you must need to understand that when the information of the complete block enters to the Merkle Tree (which we will discuss soon) it uses these Hash Functions to calculate the value of the previous block field. Another important thing which you should know is that even a difference of a space is calculated with a totally different value. Another important feature of the Hashing Algorithms is that the output value is always smaller than the input values in terms of size. Hashing Algorithms have three main requirements to be successful First it should be fast to generate output. Secondly even one value change should change the output value completely. Thirdly the output must be unique so that hash collisions can be avoided. Details of the hash collisions are out of scope of this book but still if two duplicate values are there then there will be problem.

There are many hashing algorithms being used in the computing world. These algorithm's are evolving regularly by computer scientists.

For example if we insert "How are You" in Merkle Tree for hashing and receiving "745ghdyebd4785f" as an output value, we will get "854wetvd541fnjs" a totally different value if we add an extra space "How are you". This makes it more secure. Starting with MD5 algorithm there are SHA1, SHA2, SHA3 etc. MD5 & SHA1 are quite easy to hack so both of them are deemed obsolete.

In blockchain hashing as discussed is used for security and at the same time to reduce the block size because after hashing, as discusses the valued are piped in to the Merkle Tree and then finally to to the Previous Block field of the next block.

Merkle Trees are very important part of the blockchain and they are related to the Hashing Algorithms. The merkle tree helps in validation of transactions. A Merkle Tree takes a bunch of data input and confirms its validity. Lets understand it with help of a diagram.

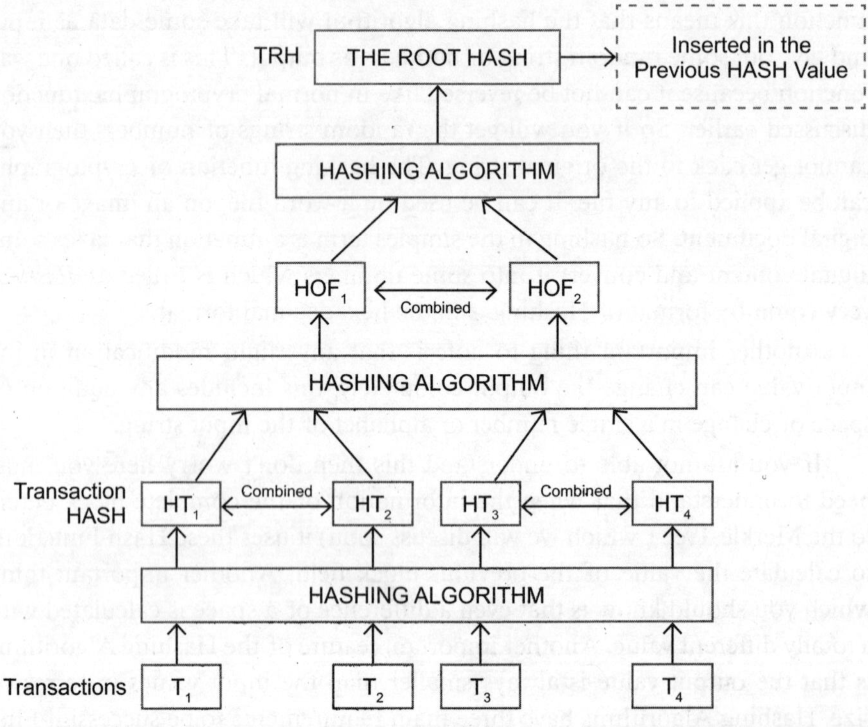

Imagine four transactions T1, T2,T3 & T4 happening in a block. Please note that although there are thousands of transactions actually happens inside a block but we took four to understand the concept clearly. All these transactions are input into a hashing algorithm to get four individual transaction hashes HT1, HT2, HT3 & HT4. Hash HT1 is combines with H2 and H3 with H4 and again fed into hashing algorithm.

The output from the second hashing algorithm we got Hashes of Hashes lets call it HOF1 & HOF2. The values of HOF1 & HOF2 are combined together to pipe in for the last time to the hashing algorithm generating an output TRH which is the Root Hash. This root Hash value is inserted in the Previous Hash value of the next block.

Every block has to go through this Merkle Tree process for providing the previous value of the next block in the blockchain. In this way this Merkle Tree provides the security and tamper proof system for blockchain. If at any stage someone tampers or changes data of a block then the whole output will change and a flag is raised by the system for an invalid value.

10
Proof of Work & Consensus in Blockchain

In the previous chapter, we have discussed the core concepts on which blockchain technology is based. You must be aware by now that a blockchain database is irreversible and once its updated with some data it will remain there for ever, till the existence of that particular blockchain. Now to understand the working mechanism of blockchain we need to put together all the concepts which we have discussed till now.

Once a Genesis Block is created, it contains some initial tokens by the developer. In case of bitcoin's the Genesis Block had 50 bitcoins to be distributed to the miners as rewards for mining more coins. When more nodes contributes to the process of mining, more block are created forming a blockchain. Each node will receive a reward for mining. As the chain gets bigger each block has a hash of the Previous Block, the first Genesis Block is the first one does not contain any value of the previous hash as it is the first one!

Lets assume that someone tampers with a block on his local computer and changed its value. (Because to join a blockchain all blockchain is downloaded on a local computer). That value is also there in the next block's previous hash value.

The blockchain system will match both values and will gets suspicious. To mitigate this scenario blockchain has a concept of proof of work. Its a mechanism which slows down the creation of the new block. This mechanism makes it very harder to tamper the block because if someone tampers a block the block hash will be recalculated by the blockchain network. Therefore changing the single value will make blockchain into self correcting mechanism to recalculate the hashes. Hashing, Proof of Work and Distributed Computing provides the security to the blockchain network. As we know that the copy of the whole blockchain is downloaded in the local computer whenever some one joins a bitcoin network for mining and also there are millions of miners across the globe. This means that we have millions of copies of the same database residing all over the world. This peer to peer network make sure to update all the copies of the world after a successful entry in the database. If someone tries to tamper with the blockchain his copy automatically gets overwritten and synchronized with the millions of copies residing in different computers on the network. In similar manner when ever a new block is created by the miners that block is copied and sent to all the computer mining nodes on the planet!

In this way consensus are maintained in the whole block chain. To tamper a particular blockchain successfully a hacker has to first tamper all the blocks in a blockchain followed by redoing the proof of work for each block and then hacker has to take control of more than 50 percent computing mining nodes on the network which is practically impossible.

By following these security measures blockchain is evolving as the open yet most secure system in the computing world today.

11

Benefits of Blockchain Technology

Invention of blockchain has resulted in tremendous potential for several industries. Some complicated problems in the world, now can be solved by using this technology. Blockchain technology has opened many avenues of research and development. Let's discuss some of the real benefits of using blockchain technology and why it is becoming popular among the big corporations and government sectors around the world.

Transparency

As discussed transparency is one of the foremost feature and benefit of using blockchain technology. Traditional database system can either be password protected or restricted completely or they can be made open to public with all identity blown. This means issues in privacy. But as the blockchain is the modern book keeping system when changes are made into the database, the changes could be seen by anyone on the network and once a database entry is added it cannot be deleted by anyone under any circumstances. Therefore developing applications by using the blockchain technology can automate many aspects of business processes and can provide transparency at the same time.

Middle Man Removal

As discussed before most of the transactions in the real world and on ***INTERNET*** requires a middle man or intermediaries who facilitates a particular transaction and earn some commission for the services. Paypal is currency payment intermediary between a sender and a receiver, Amazon is intermediary between buyers and sellers. Blockchain in a same way is an autonomous system managed by all senders and receivers removing intermediaries.

Decentralized System

Remember the chapter where we have discussed about the computer system architecture. As we know blockchain is based on a decentralized architecture and at the same time provides transparency and security. This is an important feature which can be used to consolidate big data.

Trust

We trust our banks and put our money in fixed deposits, we also deposit cash in our banks. In same way trust is very important when you deal with any system or organization. Blockchain technology so far has proved itself to be the best in terms of maintaining trust between all the parties involved in the transactions. Once you join a blockchain you can able to see all the details of the transactions in open ledger.

Security

The data in blockchain is very secured as it works on complex mathematical algorithms. It can not be changed or altered in any circumstances. It is only possible because of the trail of data it generates which is woven together in a secured an coherent way. In conventional systems the transaction trails can be altered and fraud can happen. Even after detection of a fraud it usually takes a very large amount time to trace back the fraud because the trail is usually so messed up. But in case of blockchain fraud is not possible because no one can alter that data in any circumstances. Theoretically a blockchain can be hacked only if a single person can control more than 50% of the records but this scenario is not possible because blockchain is scattered geographically and no one can control all computing resources at the same time. At the same time security is never 100 percent perfect but at least it is better than the other kind of solutions available in the market as of now.

Infinite Usage Scenarios

Blockchain technology can be used in any applications where data is used other than money. Money or cryptocurrency is one of the applications of blockchain technology. Some of the usage scenarios with cryptocurrency, smart contracts and blockchain are discussed further in this book.

Cost Reduction

Another benefit is the reduction in costs. For instance money senders need to pay very little for their transactions for transfer of money across the globe. Other than money, it can severely cut down cost of the database management as any kind of physical or digital asset can be tracked and transferred. For example Share market can run in a decentralized way, round the clock by implementing blockchain technology.

Faster Transactions & Load Sharing

Not only costs will decrease it will also in turn decrease the tact time for each transactions if implemented properly. For example currently bitcoin transaction is faster (under 10 minutes) than RTGS/NEFT which takes sometime more than 10 minutes to complete. Blockchain based cryptocurrency transactions are as fast as real time sending and receiving of payments. The computing and physical assets are distributed across the globe and hence blockchain system has load sharing capability.

As we know that every technology has its pros and cons same is with the blockchain technology. Although this technology has far more positive contribution for the mankind but still it has some risks.

Being a Digital Ledger makes it susceptible to virus and hackers attack constantly. Disclosing your private key on internet makes it very easy for someone to transfer all money into your account without a clue. The transactions based on blockchain are non reversible so there is no scope of going back or reverting it. Some wallet services and stores in case of bitcoin transactions are not secure.

12
Blockchain & World Economy

After the introduction of blockchain technology it has been adopted widely by big corporation and trade houses to develop applications based on their own requirements. US Market NASDAQ is using the blockchain technology to help with share trading. The blockchain used by NASDAQ is using pre-IPO share trades and helps in settlements of the financial transactions. Other companies like Citibank, Visa has recently invested in a blockchain company to setup a blockchain that will help them in transactions happening between different financial institutions. Ripple is another cryptocurrency designed specifically for these kinds of operation. We will be discussing ripple later in this book. Moreover 25 major banks are working with a technology company R3 for a block chain. This includes prominent financial institutions like JP Morgan and other big US banks. The technology developed by R3 is a little bit different from the blockchain technology when in they have improved the existing technical model and tweaked it for their own requirements. The Bank of England is also working towards development of their own private blockchain technology based application. Blockchain in this way has been accepted as well as rejected by many organizations and governments around the world. It is very interesting to observe the government response to this new popular technology and specially bitcoin cryptocurrency. Some governments are favoring the system and some think that it will have adverse effects on the economy in terms of tax evasions and illegal activities. United States for example has a stand where they think that most of the cryptocurrency is being used for funding terrorist activities and illegal trade. Ethereum and Coinbase cryptocurrencies are summoned by the IRS for tax evasions in United States. Bank of America one of the biggest bank of the United States has abandoned the idea of using cryptocurrencies altogether. China on the other hand is taking a different path altogether. On 8th March 2018 the People's Bank of China announced that "Digital Currency 'Inevitable', Bitcoin 'Not Accepted' As Payment". This shows that although China is very much interested in the cryptocurrencies but they are not accepting bitcoin so they might be developing their own cryptocurrency for the masses. Cryptocurrency for a huge nation like China and India can prove to be a blessing in disguise as cryptocurrency can reach to the remotest part of the country where people could not use the conventional banking services.

Switzerland's biggest bank Falcon allows their high profile client to trade in bitcoins. Falcon offers bitcoins to their client as a kind of investment instrument.

India also took a harsh step in February 2018. Finance Minister in his speech explicitly mentioned & announced Bitcoin as an illegal currency. On 9th April 2018 following the budget guidelines RBI announced and capped buying of cryptocurrency from Indian Bank accounts. This in turn resulted in a great loss to investors. But it's not end. Government reactions and policies changes with time. It is quite possible that India will also follow the China's path to launch a government backed cryptocurrency. Sooner or later experts across the globe believes that need for cryptocurrency will surpass its negative dimensions.

13 Blockchain Earning Mechanisms

As blockchain is the new technology especially for the developing countries like India. It has an enormous monetary potential. Lets investigate few avenues where one can make some money by using blockchain technology.

Funding a new Blockchain Application

For you as an investor or a general user it is not possible to make and develop your own blockchain application. This does not make your chances dull to make money in the upcoming market. The companies that are currently developing new applications needs funds to expand their operations and to sustain with the development cost. You can seed any amount you wish into a good company and when the developed application is sold, you will get your share of profit diligently. At times dividends are also shared like share markets.

Creating a New Platform

If you are tech savvy enough to supervise the development then this is the best thing you can do in current business scenario. All you need is money and good technical team. There are many companies who are looking to outsource their blockchain applications to third party. All you need a good business problem solving skill to get going.

Invest in any existing blockchain application.

You can invest in any blockchain currency including bitcoin and can get the benefits of the appreciating market value. Right now the bitcoin market is bullish and every day prices are rising. So you can trade your favorite cryptocurrency which is actually a blockchain application. We will also discuss trading options of other cryptocurrency including bitcoin in detail in later parts of this book.

Start Selling Blockchain Applications & Platforms

Some companies are providing very good commissions and incentives for the sales force to convince people to invest in their companies. In this way you can actually ask your friends or relatives to be part of the revolution to earn money. There are several referral programs being promoted by pcpular enterprises.

Other than these you can also start developing Add On's for the blockchain applications & can sell those addon's to the Internet Market Place.

In this way there are several other avenues and potential scenarios to earn money with the Blockchain Technology.

PART THREE

Bitcoin

14
Introduction to Bitcoin

Bitcoin is a sort of currency or rather a digital token which is not backed by the government of any country. The generation of this currency is fixed in the initial Genesis Block as 21 million and no more currency can be mined or generated after that. This currency is distributed and decentralized across the globe. Generation of these bitcoin is done using mining which we will discuss later in detail. The generation and validation of the transaction of bitcoin requires great computational power therefore often the mining and validation is done by collaborating power of many different nodes or computers. New coins are generated as the rewards to the miners who validate and authenticate these transactions. The job of the miners is to assemble a high end dedicated computer system and attach it with the global bitcoin mining network to contribute in the system.

Bitcoin currency is represented by BTC. As the people are trading more day by day, more computational power is needed to authenticate those high volume of transactions and at the same time the blockchain's database or ledger is also growing exponentially. Miners these days have to put in more effort interms of computational power to get more rewards from the system. The smallest denomination of a bitcoin is 1. Satoshi which is named after it's inventor. 1 Satoshi is equal to 0.00000001 bitcoin. Bitcoin is a decimal number system based currency therefore we can pay and receive bitcoins in fractions upto 8 decimal places! This makes it more powerful to use as a digital asset.

Bitcoin is a Public Ledger system or Public Blockchain and its ledger is open to access for all. Bitcoin currency is placed or stored in wallets and the buying and selling of this digital currency is facilitated by numberous on line exchanges. These exchanges take a fraction of bitcoin as a transaction fee.

As discussed bitcoin came and originated as the world's biggest digital currency which is not supported by any government institution. In our conventional monetary system all money is backed by the government or the reserve banks. These banks or reserve banks can print money according to the demand and they can increase and decrease inflation in the market. But in Bitcoin the amount of coins are fixed as 21 millions. This also means that price of this cryptocurrency will always be based on the market forces and demand and supply will be the yard stick for its market price.

People across the globe are considering bitcoin as an important instrument of investment and that is evident in its current price of over ₹ 6 lacs per bitcoin! This currency has an exponential rise after 2008. As of today not many vendors are accepting it as a mode of payments for transactions. Recently world's biggest digital money exchanger PayPal has attached bitcoin to their medium of payment for its merchants.

15
Solo Mining & Mining Pools

In the previous chapter we have touched upon the concept of rewarding the people who contribute their computational power for the validation of these transactions entries and help to distribute these entries to other computers on the blockchain network after proper authentication.

Mining can be defined as a process of generating new bitcoins by validating the ongoing transaction in the blockchain database.

Let's make it more easy to understand. As we know that a block has all the transactions entries and these entries are distributed to the other computers around the world after the authentication and we have also learned that this authentication and validation is done by using the cryptography and hashing. Therefore the computer is participating in the bitcoin is miner computer and the process is called as *Mining* and that miner will be rewarded with few bitcoins for successfully doing a job. The miner is rewarded a whole bitcoin or a fraction of it and it depends on the complexity of the problem solved or the number of blocks authenticated by the miner. These kinds of rewards attach and motivate more people to join network as a miners and more number of miners means a more computational power for the bitcoin network.

The bitcoin network is very smart its like an adaptive competitive exam of GMAT or GRE. In these tests if a student answers a right question system shows them a difficult problem and gradually the difficulty level of the test increases with each correctly answered question. In the same way bitcoin puts on a more complicated problem to solve in front of the miner to earn more coins.

Initially during the first few early years of bitcoin the mining was performed on a normal computer with a good amount of RAM and a processor. But soon the number of transactions started to increase and bitcoin's network called for more computational power. (Remember there can be thousands of transactions on a single block) for hashing functions to validate and authenticate.

Then gradually computer scientists introduced a new way of mining by using the graphics card computing power for mining. These graphics card were used by the gamers for flawless graphics in high end computer games. But sooner in 2012 the bitcoin transactions increased to a level that even the clusters of GPU's computational power was not sufficient to mine coins viably and miners across the world started to look out for other alternatives.

In 2013 some companies introduced a dedicated hardware systems specially designed for the process of bitcoin mining. These systems were called as ASIC (Application Specific Integrated circuits) cards that were programmed at the hardware level for bitcoin mining.

The ASIC cards proved to be much faster than the conventional mining hardwares in terms of computational power. But again with the rise of Silk Route web portal the popularity of the bitcoins rose like never before. The bitcoin became a global buzz word. It became so popular that the transaction volume growth had 150 percent increase over a period of few months and the ASIC cards also could not able to handle the computational load. This had an impact on the individual miners. The people who were earning handsome amount of rewards independently were not able to calculate these kind of complicated problems by using their own resources. Therefore mining as an avenue of earning money went out of their hands. To tackle this kind of crisis, miners around the world came together and pooled their computational powers to solve complicated problems collectively and this gave birth to the new concept of mining pools.

A mining pool is a group of Miners who pool in their resources and participate in the mining process. Once a transaction is verified and added into a blockchain the rewarded bitcoins are divided among all who participate in the mining process. In this way they were able to counter the ever increasing demand for computational power by the system. There are many popular mining pools that are joined by miners to mine bitcoins. Usually the reward coins are calculated after deducting a nominal pool fee imposed by the mining pool body. There are many ways in which a contribution is calculated and rewarded by the mining pool system. Pay-per-Share, Proportional, Pay-per-last-N-shares, Geometric Calculation are some of the methods. The simplest one is the Pay-per-Share (PPS) approach which offers an instant, guaranteed payout to a miner for his contribution to the probability that the pool finds a block. Miners are paid out from the pool's existing balance and can withdraw their payout immediately. This model allows for the least possible variance in payment for miners while also transferring much of the risk to the pool's operator.

Some of the most popular mining pool operators include Slush Pool, F2 Pool, AntPool, ViaBTC, BTC.com, Poolin, Genesis Mining, Bit fury, Binance Pool and Kano Pool. Joining these pools is easy and rewards are respectable.

Miners across the globe are moving towards mining other cryptocurrencies also. As the load on the bitcoin network is increasing and it is calling for more resources passing day. Miners are preferring other kind of cryptocurrencies which offer good rewards with less contribution in terms of the computational power. The Ethereum, Litecoin, Bitcoin cash are some of the other alternatives which are popular today. We will be discussing these cryptocurrencies in a separate chapter.

16
Bitcoin Wallets

A wallet is something which carries your cash physically in your pocket everyday. Cryptocurrency wallet, although not a physical wallet but it functions like exactly one. It stores the original bitcoin private keys safe and secure. One can keep all coin in his wallet after purchasing or mining. It also act as a medium of sending and receiving money with each other. Some experts classify wallets to four types – *Desktop Wallets, Hardware Wallets,Mobile wallets & Web Wallets & Some crypto experts classify them as Hardware & Software Wallets.* What ever may be the case the classification is quite simple. Web or Online wallets are the wallets that shares your personal private keys on their own cloud or servers and you can access them by using ***INTERNET*** from anywhere anytime. The most popular online wallet on Internet that is considered secure is the coinbase wallet. Daily new wallets are being introduced on Internet but one should do proper research before registration because private key is the most important thing for bitcoin its a key of a safe where all your coins are located. Private key in hands of anyone means that he has full access to your bitcoin inventory. By using private key he can transfer or use your bitcoins without ringing a bell. A comprehensive list of trusted bitcoin wallets are included in the appendix section of this book. But still it is recommended that you should do a proper study and read online reviews before subscribing any online wallet.

Storycoin is an another on line wallet which is a hybrid, because it enables user to encrypt their private keys prior to sending money to third party which increases the security of the transaction.

Trust is very important in the online wallet system because using an online wallet means hundred percent trust on the company where you are storing your private keys. As the private keys are being stored on their own servers a reputable company should be selected. Some online wallets also provides mobile devices application for iOS & Android devices.

Then another type of wallets are Desktop wallets. As it is also possible to setup a wallet on your own computer, you can actually avoid your private keys to be uploaded on third party servers or service providers. It can be down by two softwares mainly Bitcoin QT and Bitcoin core. Both of these softwares can actually create a local wallet on your desktop or laptop computer and also enables you to relay all your carried transaction on the centralized bitcoin network. This arrangement has benefit over the online wallets that your personal private keys will be stored on your local computer so you don't have to upload your keys to the third party servers on internet. But one drawback is that in case your private keys gets lost or your computer crashes down then you will never recover your money associated with these keys. Therefore one should take a proper backup of the keys in a dedicated USB drive before opting for this option. There are lot of desktop wallet providers on Internet but one of the most popular one is the Multibit. Multibit is quite simple to setup for a normal user. Armory is an another popular desktop wallet (*https://www.bitcoinarmory.com/*)

Another kind of popular wallets which are becoming quite popular are the mobile wallets. They are recommended for the mobile users who do lot of traveling. They provide the trading platform of buying and selling bitcoin on the move. These mobile wallets has enabled users across the world to pay for the goods and services on the go with a single tap on their smart phones by using the NFC or near field communication or QR codes. Mobile wallets has a very light code because mobile as a device cannot handle the whole mammoth size blockchain database because it requires a tremendous computation power. So a simplistic module is provided for basic operations on smart phone. Popular android wallet is the Hybrid Blockchain wallet Hive's. On iOS platform Blockchain Wallet & Bitcoin Wallet are the popular ones.

Then there are another kind of wallets as Hardware wallets. These wallets are device based wallets where the private and public keys are stored on a USB Hard drive or any other storage medium. Another physical medium based wallets are the ones where you can actually print your private key on paper and keep then securely in your custody. These wallets are for the long time old school type investors who want no traces of their private keys anywhere digitally.

So in this way users can choose from various types of wallets available in the market according to their preference and operational tastes. Some users prefer on line wallets over desktop wallets but the functioning aspects of all are more or less same.

17
Bitcoin Selling Buying & Exchanges (Bitcoin Trading)

We have understood till now that the private key in the bitcoin is very important array of numbers and its a secret code or a password to transact your bitcoins. Like this we have a public key which is a kind of an account number of your bank and this key is used for receiving money. As the name suggest its public so it needs to be distributed to the people for taking bitcoins. By using this public key the sender can make you payments in your bitcoin wallet.

Now we have also an understanding the every transaction in the Bitcoin world is stored on the blockchain which is called as a digital ledger or database. This database is distributed and has all the transactions records since the inception of the bitcoins. Private key should not be shared to anyone in any circumstances.

Miners also provide their public keys so that they can be rewarded bitcoins into their wallets. The main job of a miner is ιo add the transaction detail into this blockchain database and validating it as well with help of a technical prices called "*Proof of concept*". And once its validated the miner gets his reward in his bitcoin wallet. The time frame for a validation of the transaction depends on the size of the block and computational power at work from the miners end. Its approximately 30 minutes as of 2018. Usually there is no fee for the transactions and the transactions are totally anonymous. Anonymity means that the transactions performed on a portal or transfers done is hundred percent untraceable and no one can back track it to any specific person or company or the computer from which the transaction is carried out.

There are numerous exchanges present online to carry out bitcoin transactions; exchanges also facilitate users to trade buy and sell bitcoin like a commodity. Its interesting to note that bitcoin is a volatile currency. But at the same time it is heaven for intra day traders because the fluctuation in one day trade can go up to 13-14% in a single day. The biggest bitcoin exchange of the world is coinbase. One method to acquire bitcoin is to but these coins from any exchange and keep them in your wallet. Another method to get these coins is to engage in the mining process by participating in the network of bitcoin miners but this also needs investment in hardware resources and technical skills. There is one another way to buy bitcoins directly from the sellers. Sellers of bitcoin often posts their selling leads on various websites where in the buyer and seller can contact each other to close the deal. In case you are buying it from someone who has posted a selling lead online make sure to contact him first on phone so that you can talk with the actual guy before entering into any real money transaction. The usual practice of one to one buying selling is that a personal meeting is arranged at some discussed location the buyer comes there with cash and seller with his laptop in case of an online wallet. Then after counting the money the equivalent value of bitcoins are transferred to the buyers wallet. The place should be public restaurant or a coffe shop so that buyer and seller can complete the transaction after successful validation and authentication by the miners. In other words the meeting gets over after the 30 minutes proof of concept process and addition of the transaction to the blockchain network by the miners.

In case of exchange trade, In India Exchanges have started to ask for KYC before creating an account. After that they can take money via NEFT cheque or can also send individuals to your home for cash collection. But it is recommended that one should always be cautious in transacting with these companies. A thorough research work or atleast a solid reference is must before dealing with any such organization. One good valid Indian Exchange is ZebPay.

Indian Bitcoin Exchanges are not regulated or owned by the government in anyway. But still few exchanges like Bits Lamp & Karken in United states of America, OK Coin & BTC in China are managed by the governments.

The increasing world interest in the cryptocurrency in general alarmed banks who fears the loss of business as a middleman to transfer money globally. In fact still today the bitcoin is not identified as a proper currency by the governments worldwide. Therefore in case of theft of your coins you cannot file a formal complaint of a financial fraud instead it comes under the IT Act Laws of Government of India.

So, the best way to buy bitcoin currency in my opinion is to buy from an individual cautiously who post there selling leads on the country specific local websites. In India one such popular website is local bitcoins.com. In United States monthly group meeting are also held for trading bitcoins. These meetings are called "*Satoshi Squares*". In India meets are usually planned on a website www.meetup.com.

Day by Day more sellers are accepting bitcoins as mentioned previously in the book. Paypal has also started accepting bitcoin. In the same way Amazon, Subway, Expedia,Dell has also started accepting bitcoins for the mode of payment for their goods and services. Few clothing and apparel stores have also started accepting bitcoins as the mode of payment.

To find a bitcoin friendly merchant in your area you can login to *www.coinmap.org* which has a database of all stores with locations.

Some popular gambling sites has also started accepting bitcoin as mode of payments. Websites like Satoshi *Dice, Bet Coin & Peer Bet* are the popular ones. The integration of bitcoin by expedia has opened new avenues for the business. It gives extra advantage to travelers, who do not need to worry anymore about the exchange rate and conversion charges. Few flight booking portals has also started accepting bitcoins like *www.flyhigh.fi* is one of them. Another popular use of bitcoin is to purchase a gift card from retailers so that card holder can encash the retailer's gift card for products and services of his choice at their online or physical stores. Some dedicated market places have emerged that accepts cryptocurrencies for products one such popular market place is crypto thrift (*www.cryptothrift.com*) which has auctions and buy it now features like ebay.

Although purchasing items online by using cryptocurrencies especially bitcoin is quite easy from the online portals selling bitcoins or encashing them for real money is a different story and requires some serious efforts. As the price of the bitcoin is not governed by single entity the buying and selling price is exchange dependent.

Specially in Indian context many investors face regular problem to encash their bitcoins. If you remember that few moments ago we have disussed the ways in which one can purchase bitcoins. In similar manner we have three ways of selling bitcoins or converting them for real cash.

First way of selling Bitcoins are by Direct Trade. In this method seller can post his Bitcoin lot details, quantity and expected price of a forum or website like Coinbase, local Bitcoin portal. Interested buyers can contact the respective sellers can take this deal forward.

Many exchanges also facilitate the buying option of bitcoins that are sold to their members by them. These exchanges also facilitate one on one trade platform of buying and selling platform with some commission. The main difference in the direct trade and this one is that in this method exchange acts as a mediator for both buyers and sellers and they usually hold funds till the time. Bitcoins are transferred to the buyer by seller. Its a kind of buyers protection provided by Amazon & Ebay India.

Third interesting way of selling bitcoins is peer to peer trading. In this type of trade scenario if a person with bitcoins wants to buy product and services from a website or a physical store that don't support. Bitcoin as a payment method then the interested bitcoin buyer can purchase that product for the bitcoin seller by using his own debit or credit card and after the transaction bitcoin seller can transfer the equivalent amount of bitcoins into the Purchaser's Wallet.

It is interesting to note that although the bitcoin is an anonymous currency but in case of exchange trade, direct trade or peer to peer trade one can loose his identity to the other party. In case of exchanges, few exchanges asks its members to upload a government issued document for verification and in similar way during one on one trade your identity is blown.

Another recommendation for this trade is to decide the buying or selling price in advance and on paper or on email so that there will be no dispute on the actual transaction day as the price of the bitcoin fluctuates a lot. Few months back single bitcoin was 14 Lacs INR and now its just over 6 Lacs. Therefore, it is must to bind your seller or buyer with some kind of written communication.

More information about the various exchanges and their web address can be accessed in the Appendix section of this book.

18
Transition from Bitcoin to Bitcoin Cash

Bitcoin cash is an another cryptocurrency based and programmed on the lines of bitcoin. If you remember we talked about the hard and soft forks in the starting section of this book where we understood the concept of hard forked software where more of less whole code structure needs to be changed. And soft forking was just changing few parameters of the code without changing its core functionality. Now this segwith2 which we are going to discuss is the soft forking of the blockchain software.

By 2017 the popularity of bitcoin increased exponentially and so as the requirement of computational power for mining process. The miner pools and independent miners across the world tried to find a solution for fast validation and authentication of the blockchain. The immense database or the ledger size of the blockchain became bottle neck for further expansion as the investment in computational power resources surpasses the earned rewards making mining inviable for most of the miners.

Therefore, scientists came out with a solution of Segwit 2. A solution by which the block size of the blockchain could be made smaller by removing signature data. By inserting this Segwit2 code inside the blockchain core they were able to reduce the size of the block to at least 65% smaller. This 65% decrease had a direct impact on the computational power and proof of concept became faster. By this solution developers achieved the scalability of the original bitcoin blockchain system.

But soon it the team of original developers had some friction because of this new decision and they got divided into two factions. One who advocated this segwit2 hard forked system and others who opposed this measure.

The developers who opposed this soft fork claimed that even after changing a little code the core has not changed and therefore fundamentally the scalability problem still exists. They said that for this solution to work instead of a soft fork a complete hard fork is needed because the block size of the blockchain in bitcoin is only 1 MB's which is too less for the amount of transactions carried out day by day.

The those group of developers started working on a new hard fork version and changed the block size to 8 MB. Basically they have tweaked and incorporated all the limitations of the original bitcoin in their hard forked version. They named this hard forked version as "Bitcoin Cash" and it became a new currency. The Bitcoin Cash is denoted by BCC or BCH.

Some market experts even today speculates that one day in future bitcoin cash will surpass the bitcoin in terms of technical functionality and market capitalization because it is far superior in terms of scalability and robustness. At the time of writing this book one bitcoin was just over 6 Lacs Indian Rupees and One Bitcoin cash was just over 1 Lacs Indian Rupees. Now let us discuss a little bit more about the segwit2 technology and how it actually cut down the block size.

Segwit2 full form is segregated witness and as we know it was proposed as the modification of the bitcoin to make it more scalable. As we have discussed in the previous chapters that the blockchain database or the ledger of the bitcoin currency store specific transaction information and it requires large amount of space.

The initial size of the Genesis Block was 1 MB and developers tried to increase it to 2 MB by optimizing the code by soft forking and this code optimization is known as the segregated witness where developers had increased the size of the block from 1 MB to 2 MB.

Increasing the block size also has a disadvantage to the miners because increasing the block size will increase the size of the complete blockchain and it calls for more resources for mining. Whole blockchain needs to downloaded on the mining computer that inturn makes it more expensive in storage and computational power.

Developers also made an upgraded the original core of Bitcoin in 2015 and hard forked it to Bitcoin XT. This Bitcoin XT core has integrated segwit2 with increased block size for better scalability and stability. More information about this core can be accessed at *www.bitcoinxt.software*

PART FOUR

Other Cryptocurrencies

19

Dash

History

Dash was named as Xcoin when it was launched in January 2014 but again after one month is was named as Darkcoin. Again in March 2015 the Darkcoin was again changed to its present name "DASH". 25% of the coins which was about 1.9 million coins were automatically generated after the genesis block because of some little error in the initial code.

Technical Introduction

Master Nodes

As we have learned that in bitcoin all jobs are completed by the miners who gets reward from the application for successful transactions. In Dash it is little bit different because DASH uses a two tier network setup. Miner's handle the creation of the blockchain or the transactions block in the same way as bitcoin or a normal blockchain. Other than this there are another set of computer nodes called as Master Nodes. These master nodes performs various other functions related to the governance of DASH.

Like a savings bank account with minimum balance, if you want to participate as a master node the DASH network requires you to keep at least 1000 DASH coins in your wallet. You can use this amount anytime you like as there will be no restriction but your master node status will gets disabled automatically. The mining rewards are distributed evenly 45% to both miners and master nodes. Rest 10% is kept as funds to maintain the system. This is different from other cryptocurrencies usually the managing organization in other currencies are dependent on third party for their research and fund needs but DSH as a cryptocurrency is far mature from the beginning itself. They have allocated 10% funds for that from the starting.

Private Send

DASH also solves the problem of double spending problem with Instant Spend where in transactions can actually be processed in real time. Another important feature of DASH is that user can select transaction's privacy by sending money by using private send. It was also called *dark* send because the transaction is mixed with master nodes and routed with literally hundred percent anonymity. The name was changed to private send in June 2016. This pre mixing is usually done within the user's wallet. Currently DASH system only allows 1,75000 dollars. Privacy in users is made possible with help of complex algorithms where in multiple identical inputs from multiple users are combined together to pipe out multiple outputs in a single transaction.

Governing DASH

DASH is an independent decentralized system of funding as well as governance. Its one of the system that is *Sybil* attack proof. The consensus on the network and code are governed by the voting system in an autonomous way. The 10% management fund is used by DASH for the development and improvement of DASH crypto currency. Mainly the funds are used to hire new developers and sponsor integration with new platforms, exchanges and services. The amount received as the funds for governance is around 650000$ per month that is around 4.55 crore rupees per month!

Voting System

The dash voting system uses a simple formula (Yes - No votes) > (Total Votes of Masternodes x 0.1). The voting proposals are posted on *dash.org* or other websites like *DashCentral*. One can also track voting on *dashvotetracker.com* website. Voting is done by every node on the network. Master nodes only enjoy a certain amount of interest like savings bank on their collateral and a slight privilege in voting as shown in Fig. 19.1.

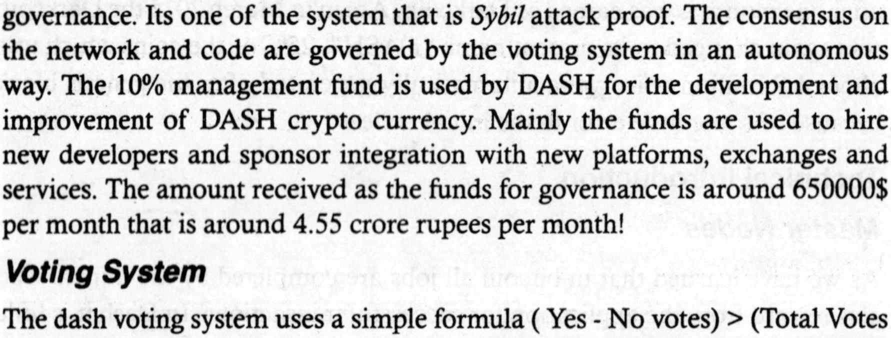

Fig. 19.1: *DASH Proposals*

Dash vote tracker website tracks detailed information about the proposals, votes status and other important information. You should login once to check the statistics as it is highly recommended. After Bitcoin we personally think that this DASH currency is the one to look out for.

In recent times there has been high speculative activity in the market. Margin trading is also being done aggressively by investors world wide. One another reason is the high price of bitcoin in recent times. People have started looking for various other cryptocurrencies in anticipation of earning profit.

Bitcoin Talk a popular forum members are quite actively participating in the mining, development and discussion activities on the DASH sub forum. This also signifies its importance to some extent. Going by the stats there are more than 6700 pages and 9 million page views related to DASH on Bit Talk Forum.

Popular DASH Wallets

1. Core Wallet

Core wallet is a complete DASH wallet with all functionality and includes a down-loadable copy of the complete DASH blockchain. Its also called as "DASH Core" or "QT" Wallet. To download this wallet you need to visit *www.dash.org* and click on the download section of the website. One important hing to remember this wallet is that its very heavy size and it requires a lot of time for syncronization with the DASH Blockchain Network.

2. Electrum Wallet

Electrum wallet is quite opposite to the QT wallet. It is a very light based wallet which do not require a whole blockchain on personal computer to run. Receiving and sending funds are also very easy. It is also available on *www. dash.org's* download section.

3. DASH Paper Wallet

As discussed in the bitcoin section, Paper Wallet are for the old school people who want to invest money in DASH and want to keep all their personal keys in the physical locker. DASH paper wallet generation is very simple by using the services of *www.walletgenerator.net*. This website provides a stand alone zip program to generate a wallet. Steps are easy and intuitive. With few clicks you can create your paper wallet. Don't forget to disconnect INTERNET while using the program for maximum privacy and security.

4. Exodus - Web Wallet

Exodus wallet is the most popular web wallet for DASH. This wallet is quite secure as the private keys are generated and stored on your personal computer. It can be configured by visiting *www.exodus.io*

Cryptocurrency Credit Cards

There are some popular cryptocurrency debit card providers in the market. Shake Pay (*www.shakepay.co*) and Spectro coins (*www.spectrocoin.com*) are most popular ones. These cards can be topped up with a cryptocurrency and supports an automatic conversion at merchant shops. For example if you want to buy something with these cards while making payments the cryptocurrency will automatically gets converted in USD and will be delivered to the shopkeeper's account in real time. The conversion and transactions are real time and buyers can take advantage of the fluctuating USD rates.

Faucets

Faucets were developed by Gavin Andresen in 2010. It is a reward system often hosted on a website or coded in the mobile application where in users are awarded some amount of coins for their interaction. Some cryptocurrencies have promoted their coins by using this marketing strategy. So it can also be a way other than mining to generate cryptocurrency on Internet. Users can make some DASH coins by visiting *www.dash-faucet.com*. This website provides some dash coins after every 60 minutes. *www.dashfaucet.net* is an another website which is also popular among DASH traders and investors. This website also shows with drawl information on its page.

For starting this method is quite easy to get into the world of cryptocurrencies. *www.dash.makejar.com* is a website which has a comprehensive list of the latest available faucet's and their payout's.

Mining DASH

As we know that the process of mining is used to generate new coins and also nodes are rewarded for authenticating and processing a successful transaction in the database. DASH uses X11 algorithm, which is solved by the miner's computers to receive rewards from the system. The wonderful thing about DASH is that it still support all kind of hardware for mining. CPU,GPU & ASIC mining. DASH also supports Pool Mining. One of the most popular pool mining used by DASH users is Nice Hash (*www.nicehash.com*).

Buying & Selling DASH

Dash Nearby web portal provides buying and selling services to the DASH investors. You can visit *www.dashnearby.com* for more details. Its an online marketplace for DASH and facilitates meeting of buyers and sellers in same geographic region and locality. *Poloniex.com* is one of the most popular exchange where one can buy DASH online. It also supports many other popular cryptocurrency.

The current value of 1 DASH is approx 30,000 INR.

20
Litecoin (LTC)

Litecoin is based on segwit 2 which we have discussed in bitcoin section of this book. It was developed by Charlie lee who developed this cryptocurrency in 2011 while working for Google. In 2017 he left his job and joined hundred percent for developing Litecoin. It is currently the fourth biggest cryptocurrency after Bitcoin, Ethereum, DASH Coin. Litecoin's main focus is on adaptation of this coin by more and more exchanges, merchants and users. Litecoin can be considered as a lite and improved version of bitcoin with improved performance.

Litecoin vs Bitcoin

Speed

Litecoin transactions usually took 2.5 minutes to complete. Bitcoin is around 15 minutes. This means that block processing is very fast in litecoin which helps in better processing. Although faster processing speed means more orphaned blocks during the process of mining but it provides security to the Double spending attack which is prominent in bitcoin because of the more processing time. Litecoin requires around 10 times less computation power than bitcoin.

No of Coins in Genesis Block

Remember when we discussed about the economy with a fixed number of currency and bitcoin has initially 21 million coins that can ever be created? In similar way litecoin value in its genesis block is 84 million. Only 84 million coins can be generated ever in litecoin.

Algorithms

Bitcoin uses SHA 256 for hashing which means the development cost for the ASIC boards will be quite less compared to litecoin which uses complicated scrypt algorithm.

Mining

Litecoins a can be mined with help of GPU or 3D cards. CPU mining could be done but its treacherous for the system. Solo mining is not viable as pool mining because of the rising popularity. AMD 3D cards are more popular than NVDIA for mining lite coins. When litecoins are produced a block header is hashed. The structure of the Block header is kind of similar as bitcoin which we have discussed earlier in this book. Miners are rewarded around 20 litecoins per block however this amount will be reduced or halved every four years. *www.litecointalk.io/c/*mining is the popular forum to start with mining. This forum has everything to dive into mining straight away!.

Wallets

Litecoin QT is the most popular wallet used by many investors. It is a desktop based wallet. As in desktop wallet all your private and public keys will be store on your personal computer system. You need to download this wallet on your system first to use it. Another popular Web Wallet is Lite Address Wallet (*www.liteaddress.org*). Coinkite is a Canada based wallet services company which is quite secure and reliable. (*www.coinkite.com*). They might charge you premium for their outstanding services but its worth it. The main advantage to their client they provide is the hybrid online & offline services are synchronized with the trading time. Your private keys will be accessible on internet only when you are about to make transactions. Most of the virus and hackers attack happens only when market is offline. Therefore it is a kind of security one needed to store their keys. All wallets can be encrypted and can be configured to enter password or a pin before a transaction which can provide another layer of security to your cryptocurrency.

Some other popular Litecoin wallet's are Coins Desk (*www.coinsdesk*), Electrum () & CoinsBank, Litevault (*www.litevault.net*)

Buying & Selling Litecoin

There are number of online exchanges that support litecoin trading. (*www.litecoinlocal.net*) is a portal that connect local buyers and sellers geographically. You can meet sellers personally and can carry out cash transactions. Coinbase online exchange is the most popular exchange among traders. (*www.coinbase.com*) You need to create a verified account with your Aadhar Card and Pan Card and then after proper verification you can start trading in litecoin. Kraken is another popular exchange (*www.kraken.com*). It is similar to coinbase, creation of account might take some time but its quite simple. You can start trading in litecoins in 15 minutes.

Litecoin's current market capitalization is around 3 billion USD and price of one litecoin is under 11200 INR/Coin.

21
Ethereum, Ripple & Monero

As the bitcoin is becoming more difficult to mine and its price has reached beyond purchasing power of a common man. Computer professionals across the globe are looking for another alternatives in cryptocurrency arena. Here are some of the contenders that are capable of giving competition to the bitcoin popularity.

Ethereum

The first one in our list is ethereum. It is another blockchain implementation on which ethereum cryptocurrency is based. Some people call the currency as ethereum as well but both of them are on of the same things and are correct. ethereum is the second largest cryptocurrency being used and traded in the world just after bitcoin. The ethereum was launched in July, 2015 and uses C++ platform for its development. The functioning of the blockchain is similar to the bitcoin's blockchain and is based on open ledger or open database concept. Mining and proof of work are used in similar way in the implementation of this block chain. Authentication and validation of transactions are performed in similar fashion as in bitcoin.

In the beginning of 2016 Hackers around the globe launched a month long attack on the ethereum network where in the hackers were able to access the 50 million dollars fund. After this incident the core team of developers decided to change and modify its code and in 2017 they hard forked it to launch a new ethereum. Simultaneously the developers have renamed the original ethereum as "*ethereum classic*" and the new hard forked version as "*Ethereum*". The ethereum classic is now "ETC" and ethereum is (ETH).

Fundamentally ethereum is far superior in technology than the primitive Bitcoin. The smart contracts in the ethereum blocks can be implemented easily and can provide the robust solution to various business problems. Another major advantage of ethereum blockchain is that it supports other applications to run on the blockchain platform other than cryptocurrencies.

This essentially means that the developers can program a true decentralized, distributed application by using ethereum blockchain. We will be discussing more applications of this in a separate chapter in this book.

Ethereum is coded in C++ and which is widely used and user friendly programming language. Applications can be developed with faster time frames. ethereum's mining also doesn't require a special hardware or ASIC device like in Bitcoin because its core is device independent and needs comparably less computation power for validation and authentication.

Today "*Ethereum Classic*" & "*Ethereum*" has a separate set of developers who are working independently for development of both these currencies but majority of the developers are moving to "Ethereum" with every passing day. Ethereum also uses a ghost protocol and because of this mining with pooled resources or "pool mining" is not possible with this cryptocurrency. Another major difference with bitcoin is that the amount of coins to be generated are unlimited in "Ethereum" therefore some people believes that ethereum can become the currency of the future. The current price of the Classic ethereum is 1700 INR/Coin & Ethereum is 53,000 INR/Coin.

Ripple

Ripple is an another popular cryptocurrency which works on a totally different platform than blockchain technology. It has its own ripple network in which mining is not possible. Its a consensus based network and developed to be used by big corporations, banks and other financial institutions.

Multi national corporations can use the ripple network for commodity trading or to transfer any funds or assets like gold copper diamond etc. It is quite similar to the traditional or conventional monetary system. Ripple system is a kind of a debt system to the conventional money system. You can compare the ripple system with the paypal, master card or visa. It is intermediary system based on the distributed and decentralized philosophy used in the Block chain. Ripple is denoted by XRP & Current value of Ripple is 57 INR/Coin.

Monero (XMR)

The Monero is a total anonymous cryptocurrency in which transactions are untraceable. Even in bitcoin the open ledger is available to access by anyone but in Monero there is no access to ledger as well. No one can trace the trail of the coins in anyway in this particular cryptocurrency. Transactions in this cryptocurrency is 5 times faster than bitcoin. This is the only currency using the dynamic block size hence scalability will not be an issue in future also. The market capitalization of Monero is around 14 Billion USD and price of 1 XMR is 15200 INR.

PART FIVE

Laws, Legislations & Other Uses

22

Legal Aspects & Tax Laws

Everyday people perform trade in cryptocurrency markets to book profit and loss. For some people today intra day in cryptocurrency has become their bread and butter. The high returns of over 30 percent in a single day because of high volatility makes this market lucrative for many investors. In this chapter we will try to understand the tax assumptions and the American ETFA act. We will also touch upon the illegal trade and practices carried out with cryptocurrency and also try to understand the reasons for govt. Sanctions and hard stature towards bitcoin.

Bitcoin provides new billion airs for society. 150 bitcoins if brought in 2007 are 150 crore rupees of today. Imagine the rate of growth and appreciation. The people who started mining initially became opulent rich today. Their rags from riches story was possible because of the great demand and exponential price rise.

As so much money is involved in the cryptocurrency and trade was happening across the globe, governments found it difficult to tax or control the transactions. The cross world trade without any single controlling authority calls for new kinds of legislations and laws to deal with the new situation. Recently many countries including India have declared bitcoin as illegal. Few months back there was no clarity from the government. The moment government took the stand on declaring bitcoin as an illegal currency its price came down from 14 Lacs to 6 Lacs which is more than 50 percent depreciation.

As some governments across the world declared this currency as illegal and in most of the countries its legislation status is not clear, citizens and investors finds it difficult to file tax on the earned profit after investments in cryptocurrency.

But as a general practice across the world if any one is engaged in mining and earning money by investing in the hardware and resources to contribute to the blockchain then generally its not taxable and people engaged in this trade are not filing any kind of returns on this earned income.

Till today also there is no transaction tax on the transfer of bitcoin from one wallet to another or in other words if you are sending some Bitcoin to your friend then you will not be taxed on that amount.

Even receiver in this scenario is not liable to pay any tax. It is also interesting to note that even the buying of bitcoin or any other cryptocurrency from the exchange also don't calls for any kind of tax liability. Exchanges do charge a nominal fee for arranging bitcoins in your wallet but its not a kind of tax to be paid to government.

Even exchanges around the world are not liable to pay any kind of tax for conversions this means that if you are exchanging bitcoin with Indian Rupee or USD then also it is a non taxable transaction.

Now lets discuss some transactions where people are paying taxes. Like we have discussed before that bitcoin trading markets some how behaves like NSE/BSE stock market in some ways and when you buy a share and sells it at a profit, this kind of transaction is generally taxed. In similar manner the profit on the bitcoin trading is taxed as a capital gain. The rate of this tax depends on the country specific tax regulations. In bitcoin market suppose you invested 4 lac rupess and sold it for 6 lac rupees then you need to pay the capital gain tax on the 2 lac rupees profit. Usually its calculated on similar lines irrespective of the geographic location of the investor.

Selling goods by using cryptocurrency is also taxable. Therefore if any seller is accepting bitcoin to sell some product then the seller is liable to pay tax to the government in form of indirect tax.

The main reason probably for not providing any guidelines for tax filling in case of cryptocurrency trade and profit is that government around the world are not sure about the future of cryptocurrencies. Moreover cryptocurrencies are being used for illegal activities on large scale.

In fact the popularity of bitcoin as a cryptocurrency increased many folds after the launch of an online portal called "*Silk Route*". This portal is hosted on the dark web and is a heaven for the criminals and other anti social elements. Since its inception the on line market place is used to acquire guns, drugs, ammunition,narcotics etc. Other activities and services on this website includes the child pornography,live access to torture videos. This portal has also being used for hiring assassins or contract killers, kidnappers,terrorists or other kind of espionage contracts which are usually paid by bitcoin currency.

For example some one can hire a contract killer on line through this portal and can make payment via cryptocurrency which is a decentralized, distributed and anonymous and literally untraceable so practically it is impossible to trace back the details of the deal because of very high security standards and hashing algorithms being used.

Infact sites visited and hosted on dark are also anonymous and secure and very difficult to track.

One of the reason that why United States of America is against bitcoin is because according to the EFTA Act that was passed in 1978 by Jimmy Carter. An electronic transaction should always be reversible and this is one of the essential feature of an electronic transaction. It is clearly started in the legislation that if an electronic transaction is not reversible then its not a valid transaction.

But as we know in bitcoin and almost in all cryptocurrencies the transactions once done are irreversible because there is no single body governing the transactions and the sender and receiver details are concealed. Therefore bitcoin is deemed as illegal money according to US government.

If we talk about the Indian context then till last month there was no clarity on the bitcoin and other cryptocurrency status. But recently the fate of the bitcoin status has been decided and because of this many investors stepped down and sold their bitcoins. On 1st February 2018 in the announced Union Budget explicitly it was started.

"The government does not consider cryptocurrencies as legal tender or coin and (will) take all measures to eliminate the use of crypto assets...," he said while presenting the Union Budget 2018-19 in the Lok Sabha.

It was a good answer to the people who believed and speculated that Indian Politicians have stacked up their money in this cryptocurrency and attribute this as a reason for an exponential price rise after demonetization or 500 & 1000 rupees notes.

After the ban on cryptocurrency in India RBI has stopped validating the transition related to cryptocurrencies as a whole. Zeb pay, India's largest bitcoin exchange has shut down its operation completely.

In the current scenario, many exchanges and traders have approved various courts, including the supreme court of India to get relief but as of now all the efforts proved to be futile and the overall future of cryptocurrencies as a mode of transition seems gloomy as far as Indian economic scenario is concerns.

It has also been observed that few cryptocurrency currently planning to route and trade using Singapore route to redeem and buy new bitcoin but still there is no clarity on the proposed methods as no method currently is backed by the government authorities.

It is advisable to the users to hold their purchased bitcoins because the bitcoin market is under pressure till the time it is approved by RBI and other government organisations. Indian market is expected to be under pressure.

23
Other Uses of Cryptocurrency and Blockchain Technology

Till now in this book we have gone through the various aspects of both the blockchain technology and bitcoin. We have tried to answer various kind of questions related to the functioning, price determination,working,legal aspects,scalability issues and other various cryptocurrencies. In this chapter we will try to discuss the future pospects and some various domains where the blockchain technology can be used with a cryptocurrency to revolutionize the Business or Government functioning in various domains.

Lets start with Education first.

Education

Education is a very important for our personal lives, the credentials earned are there associated with us for our lifetime. We earn those credential in our elementary school followed by high school college, post graduation and in other various stages of our career. We also get awards, recommendations and certificates from various organizations for any kind of recognition or excellence in academics or at workplace. These credentials or documents are very precious and we often keep them in safe custody at our home or preferably in bank lockers.

They are also required in case of job change or higher qualification, where we submit them in photocopy and generally the originals are required at the time of admission or joining.

Managing and carrying these documents can be revolutionize by using blockchain technology.

Lets see How?

We can create a global network to track the grades of the students world wide powered by blockchain technology!!

As it is distributed the major benefit of using this that in case of a closure of a university or institute the records uploaded on the blockchain will remain forever. Authentication and validation could be done by the blockchain networks and use of this technology can stop the forgery of mark sheets and degrees.

Attendance Records

In similar manner attendance records can be updated on the blockchain automatically with device synchronization and can be accessed by the organizations for background check. For instance employer can track the punctuality to office or institute.

Refugee Database

In case of refugee arrival it has been observed that majority of them arrives without proper documentation and academic credentials to the new countries. Specially people arrive from Iran and other Middle-East Countries. A centralize degree and certificate system based on blockchain can ensure access to their education or academic credentials from any where in the world. It can help them getting their jobs based on their qualifications in the new migrated country.

Teacher's Result

Teachers result can be updated on a centralized blockchain so that in case of any lecturer seeking employment in the new university can be accessed in their performance with respect to the attendance data and students results uploaded on the blockchain database.

Even a single central database of blockchain can be built where all institutions across the globe can update this database with the students marks and certificates.

Let's discuss a scenario. Suppose Amit and Rahul are passed out from the same institution. Both of them took loans of 4 lacs from the government for their education. After completing their education they joined two different companies. The rate of interest promised by both of them to bank was 12% yearly. Amit started earning 50 thousand a month and Rahul got a job for 20 thousand a month.

With help of blockchain technology we can create a kind of economic system that can identify earning powers of both and can adjust the lending or re payments installment based on earnings. This kind of dynamic floating lending rate system for education can be established by using the revolutionary blockchain & cryptocurrency technology.

Supply Chain

The concept of the blockchain can be used in the supply chain operations it can help the warehouses to track the location of the products in logistics operations and distribution. The sending and receiving nodes can update the status in the blockchain that can be accessed by the end users or the consumers of the products. Food products manufacturing can be included in its ambit where each produced item like jam, meat etc can be tagged and updated at every production shop or during the each stage of the manufacturing process. A juice manufacturing company can first add the details of the consignment of oranges arrived at their unloading facility and then can update the peeling details followed by the juice extraction, packaging and supplying to the markets.

Consumers can access that blockchain over the network to find out the exact day and date of manufacturing of a particular can of juice. In this way more transparency and accountability could be enforced for the safety and awareness of the consumers.

Health Insurance Usage

Blockchain technology in future can impact the health care industry like never before. A centralized government backed blockchain can be created and can be linked with aadhar number with medical records of each individual including the prescriptions,tests conducted and other vital details.

Doctors on the other hand can update the outcome of their visit and diagnosis on the same blockchain ledger.

Hospitals can update the admission status of the patients and the details of the treatment into the same blockchain.

This blockchain can integrate all the health aspects of an individual. The patient will not have to carry his reports to each and every hospital during consultation.

Doctors can login to the system and can access all history and details of the patients easily. This will enable in the fast delivery of medical services to the critical injured patients where entering aadhar card number can give all information in case of accident or natural calamity. One can move freely to the country and can get all his reports whenever required.

Imagine that you fell ill during your official or business trip and you visited the doctor and he asks for your aadhar number and get all your past medical history on his computer. He recommended few tests in the local pathological lab and simultaneously updated the system. You paid his fees by using your Bitcoins and then walked into the near by lab. Again the receptionist asks you for your aadhar card and she got a copy of your previous blood test for comparison and for drafting a report.

Legal/Law & Order

All the court verdicts and judgments and each session of the courts can be recorded and updated on a centralized law ministry blockchain. It can provide more streamline governance. The uploaded judgement's on the blockchain are the fool proof system which can reduce corruption and increase transparency. The records can be linked to the previous crime records database and employers can also access it for background check.

So in this way the blockchain technology along with a centralized cryptocurrency can actually touch the lives of the people world wide with endless possibilities. It is indeed a boom to the existing world order.

PART SIX

Practical Applications

24
Creating Wallet & Personalized Bitcoin Address

To create a new Bitcoin Address all you need a computer with Internet Access. Open any web browser on your computer. (Microsoft IE, Google Chrome) and enter *http://bitaddress.org*

Entering this in your address window and pressing enter will open a webpage like this.

This web page requires java to run. In case you are not seeing a web page like this then you need to install java in your computer system. You can type "Install Java" in on your google.com page and follow rest of the steps.

Look at the figure carefully. The process of address creation has reached 41%. The page is asking you to enter some random characters in the white text box or it is asking you to move your mouse pointer. The green dots on the screen is the areas where you have moused your mouse pointer. As we have learned that it requires complex mathematical code and no single wallet address can resemble with other address, The system is calculating and generating a new address with a large number string which is starting with number 7and ending with number 9. Entering a random number or moving your mouse cursor will change this array of numbers because in that case the number in the white box will be included in the hashing function. Mouse pointers in computer system works on a specific position on screen on x and y axis. Current pointer position is inserted in the calculations and when user moves the cursor all corresponding values are taken while calculating the hash making it a more secure address.

When the process is successfully completed you will encounter a page with two QR codes.

These two QR codes are your public and private keys. Remember the chapter where in we have discussed that the Public key is the key which is used to receive money. And private key is a secret code which is required to send money. The share key is your Public Key and Secret key is your Private key. Note the string of numbers underneath each QR codes. This is the actual key.

This text is written under the screen which explains more about the Wallet & Keys.

"A bitcoin wallet is as simples a single pairing of a bitcoin address with its corresponding bitcoin private key. Such a wallet has been generated for you in your web browser and is displayed above.

To safeguard this wallet you must print or otherwise record the bitcoin address and private key. It is important to make a backup copy of the private key and store it in a safe location. This site does not have knowledge of your private key. If you are familiar with PGP you can download this all-in-one HTML page and check that you have an authentic version from the author of this site by matching the SHA256 hash of this HTML with the SHA256 hash available in the signed version history document linked on the footer of this site. If you leave/refresh the site or press the "Generate New Address" button then a new private key will be generated and the previously displayed private key will not be retrievable.

Your bitcoin private key should be kept a secret. Whomsoever you share the private key with has access to spend all the bitcoins associated with that address. If you print your wallet then store it in a zip lock bag to keep it safe from water. Treat a paper wallet like cash.

Add funds to this wallet by instructing others to send bitcoins to your bitcoin address.

Check your balance by going to *blockchain.info* or *blockexplorer.com* and entering your bitcoin address.

Spend your bitcoins by going to *blockchain.info* and sweep the full balance of your private key into your account at their website. You can also spend your funds by downloading one of the popular. Bitcoin P2P clients and importing your private key to the P2P client wallet. Keep in mind when you import your single key to a bitcoin P2P client and spend funds your key will be bundled with other private keys in the P2P client wallet. When you perform a transaction your change will be sent to another bitcoin address within the P2P client wallet. You must then backup the P2P client wallet and keep it safe as your remaining bitcoins will be stored there. Satoshi advised that one should never delete a wallet."

As mentioned in the text you can check the balance of your bitcoin wallet by visiting *www.blockchain.info* website. If you can observe this webpage has several tabs on top with Tabs Single, Paper, Bulk, Brain etc.. Clicking on each tab can genere a new kind of wallet. We have already discussed the Paper Wallet for the old school people and Brain wallet for someone who wants to remember his private or public keys.

The last tab on this screen is Wallet Details. You can enter your wallet's private key here to get all details about the corresponding QR codes and Public Keys.

Once a wallet is created you can start doing transaction by using your keys. In the similar way you can create a hardware, Desktop & Mobile wallets. Some of the reliable wallet system services are mentioned with links in the appendix section of this book. We have discussed a kind of web based wallet in this chapter. In similar manner, you can create a wallet by using the refereed services very easily.

25
Creating a Dash Wallet

As discussed previously there are many kinds of DASH wallets available on internet, which can be used to carry out transactions. In this chapter we will create a Keystone Wallet with a web browser. It is a file based wallet system.

Step 1. Go to www.mydashwallet.org

Step 2. A web page will open.

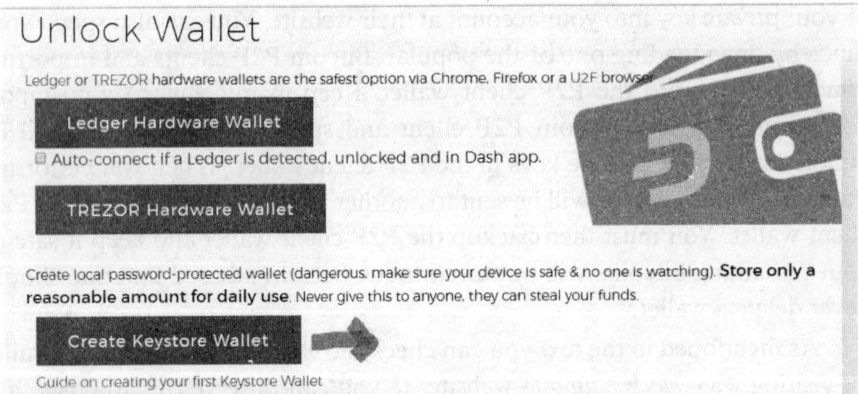

Here you need to select the kind of wallet you want to create. We will be clicking on the Create Keystone Wallet. In case you need more information about the wallet then you can read the guide. (Highlighted Yellow) or straight away click on the create Keystone wallet. We tested using Google Chrome browser currently.

Step 3. After clicking create wallet a new webpage will open.

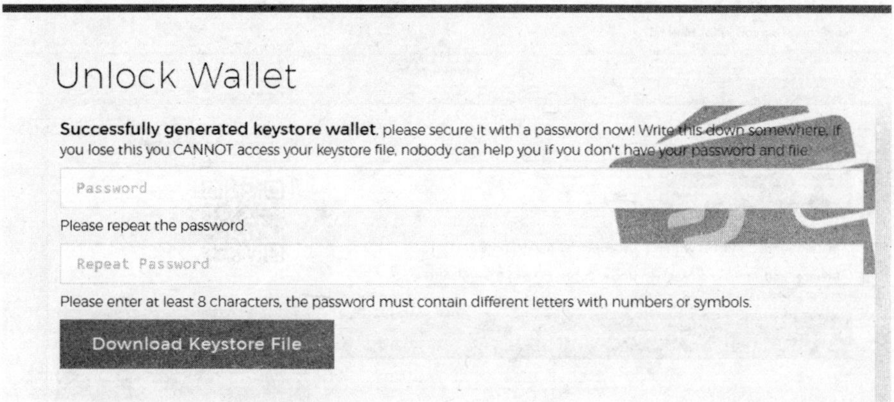

Here you need to enter a secured password you want for your wallet. The password should have a special character and mix of Capital and Smaller Alphabets and some numbers with a special character. Enter your password in both the fields and click on the download Keystone File.

Step 4. After clicking on the clock download keystone file a small size will be downloaded on the left hand side on the web browser or in the downloads folder.

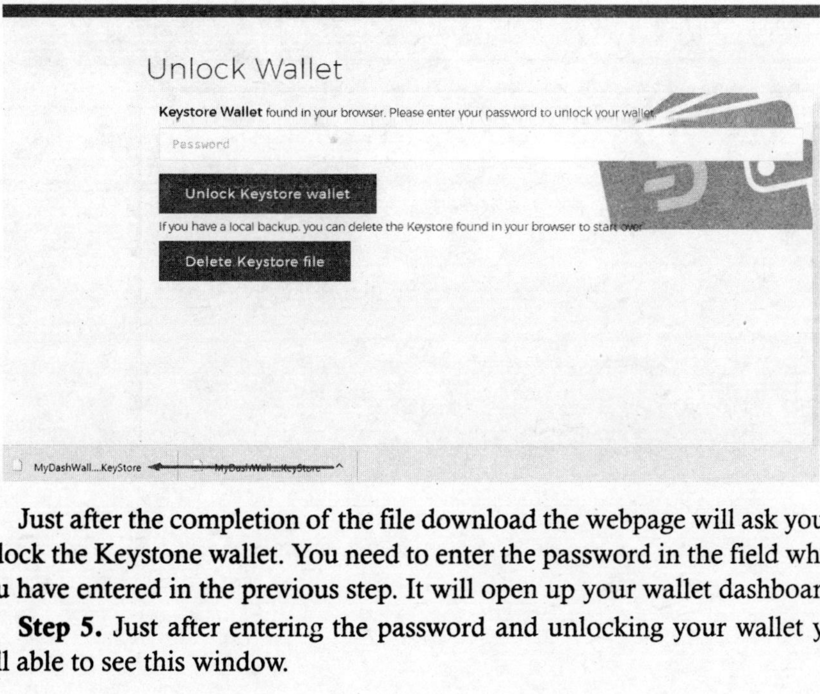

Just after the completion of the file download the webpage will ask you to unlock the Keystone wallet. You need to enter the password in the field which you have entered in the previous step. It will open up your wallet dashboard.

Step 5. Just after entering the password and unlocking your wallet you will able to see this window.

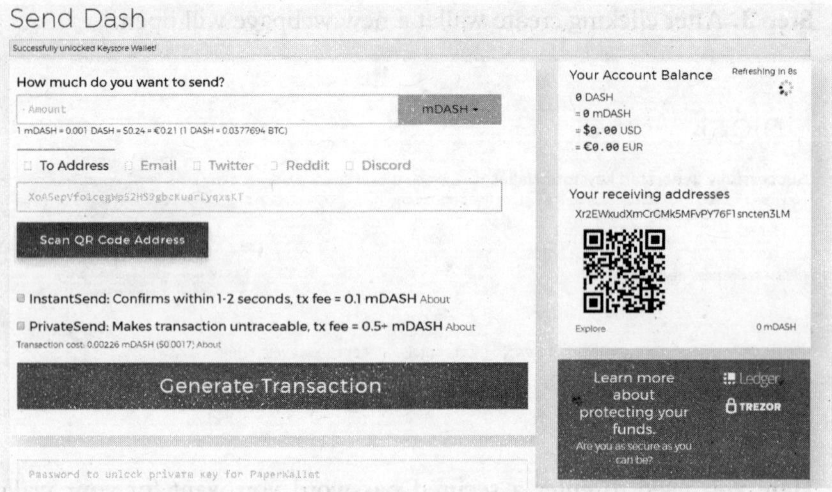

On this web page, your wallet address is on the right hand side just before the QR code. You can also send money to someone. Also note the options to send instant or untraceable Private send function. You can also print the private key by entering your password again on the same webpage.

Sending and receiving is very easy you just have to enter the sender's address or QR code to send DASH.

26
Creating a Litecoin Wallet - Electrum

In this chapter we will try to create an Electrum Wallet to trade Litecoins.

Step 1. Go to *www.electrum-ltc.org*.

Step 2. Click on Downloads and select your platform.

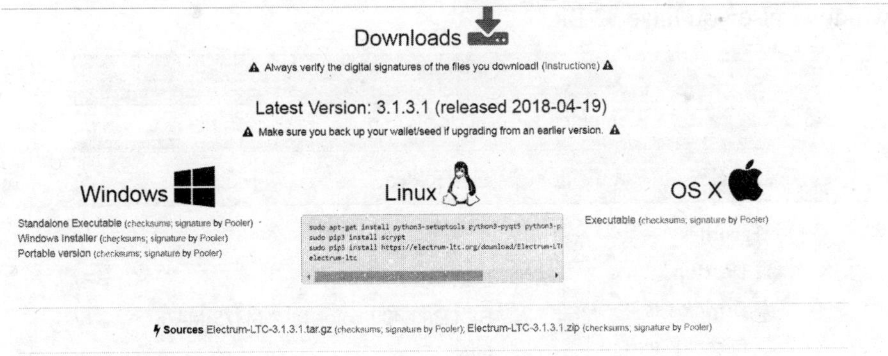

Step 3. Select your platform and a new window will open.

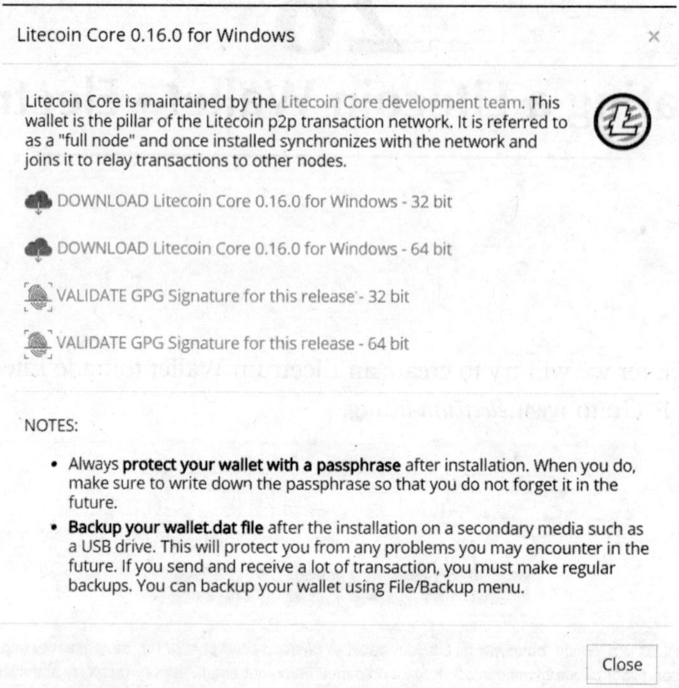

Step 4. Now select your version of windows if you are not sure. The simplest way to check is to click on my computer and go into the C Drive. If you have two program files folder like these then you have a 64 Bit version of windows else you have 32 Bit.

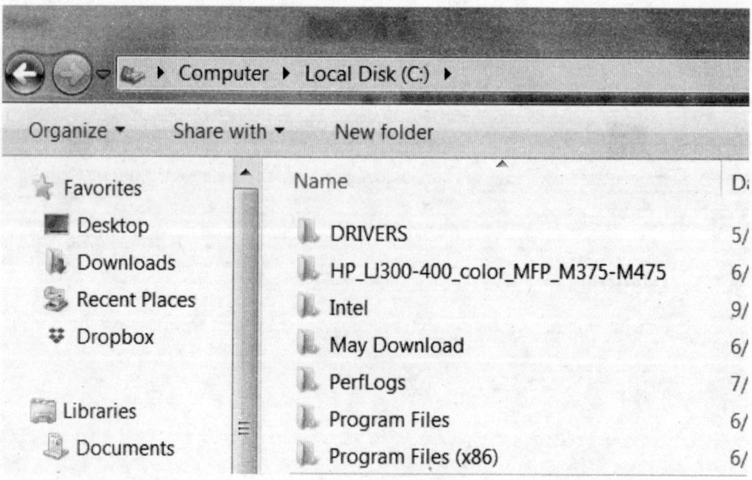

Click on the required version. Its an approximately 14 MB file.

Step 5. Double click on the downloaded file, It will start the installation process. Remember we are downloading full node of Litecoin on to the desktop there you will be requiring approx 17GB disk space. After double clicking the file click on next.

Installation Progress.

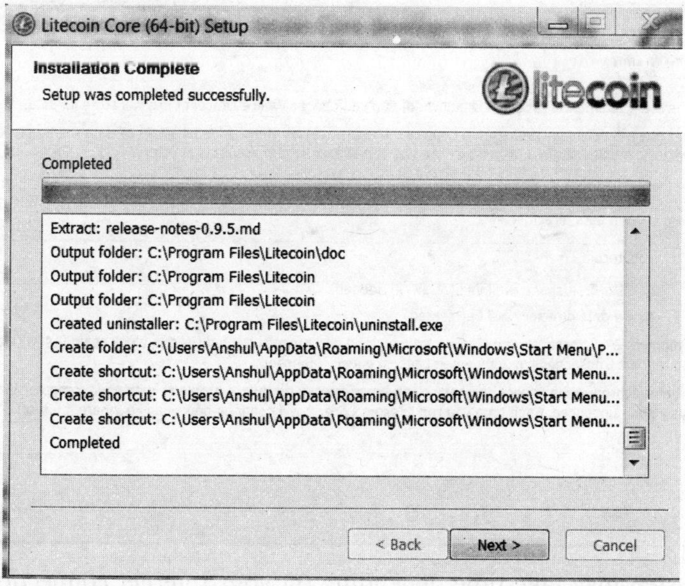

After installing and clicking next you need to run the program by clicking on finish bottom.

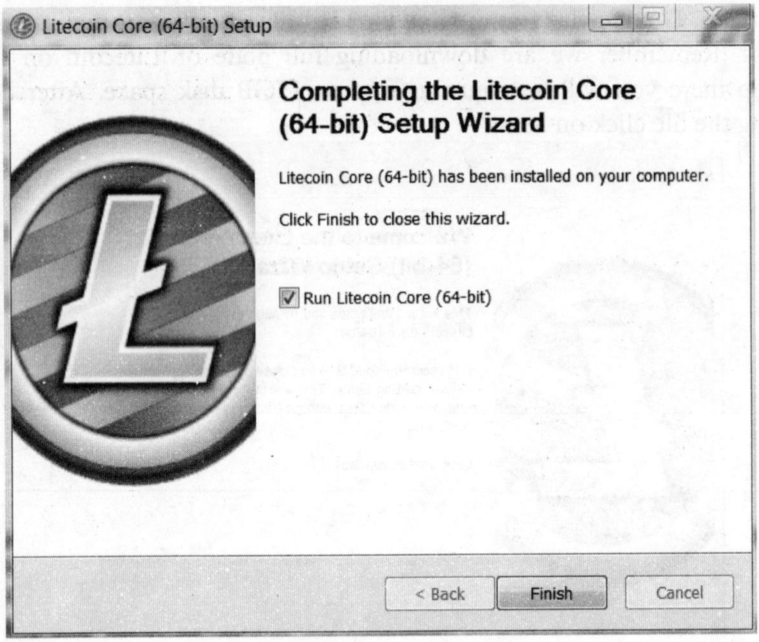

Step 6. The moment you click on finish you need to tell the program to save the complete block chain. Here we have selected F:/ as the installation directory.

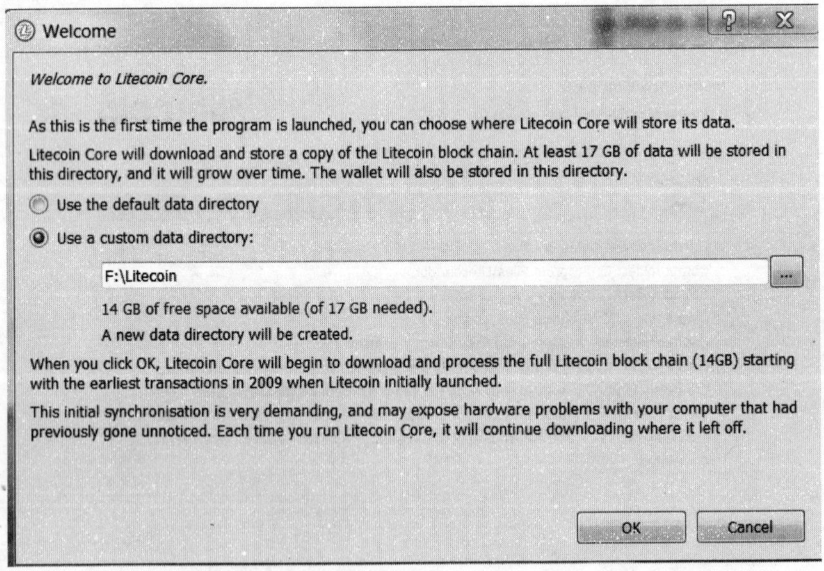

This step may take time depending on your Internet connection speed. After specifying the download address a new window will inform the download status of the block chain.

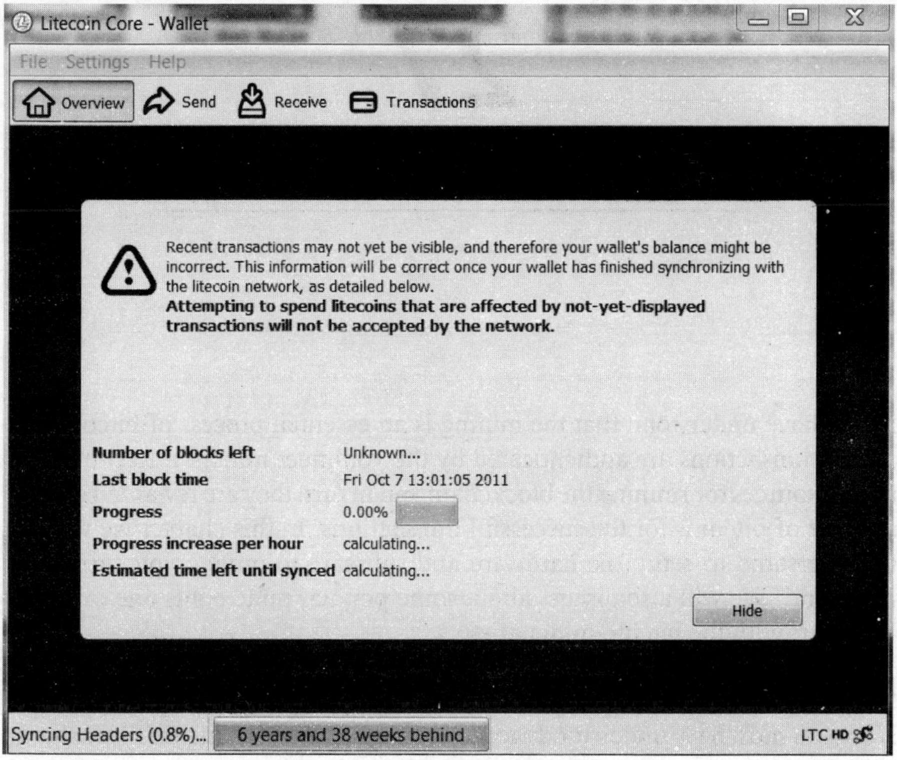
Litecoin Core - Wallet
File Settings Help
Overview
Send
Receive
Transactions
Recent transactions may not yet be visible, and therefore your wallet's balance might be incorrect. This information will be correct once your wallet has finished synchronizing with the litecoin network, as detailed below.
Attempting to spend litecoins that are affected by not-yet-displayed transactions will not be accepted by the network.
Number of blocks left Unknown...
Last block time Fri Oct 7 13:01:05 2011
Progress 0.00%
Progress increase per hour calculating...
Estimated time left until synced calculating...
Hide
Syncing Headers (0.8%)...
6 years and 38 weeks behind
LTC HD

27
How to Join a Bitcoin Mining Pool

As we have understood that the mining is an essential process of bitcoin and all the transactions are authenticated by the volunteer miners who contribute their resources for running the blockchain and in turn they are rewarded certain amount of bitcoins for the successful transactions. In this chapter we will try to understand to setup the hardware and software to mine cryptocurrencies in general. We will also discuss about some popular mine pools one can join. Lets start with the bitcoin mining first.

Bitcoin Mining

Now you must have understood the technology behind the Bitcoin Blockchain. Initially the computational power required to mine bitcoins was very less and it could be achieved by using a single computer with a good NVDIA or AMD graphic card with good memory. The popularity of bitcoin increases multiple fold over the period of time and today the transactions are happening globally in large numbers. The computational power requirements are also on its peak and bitcoin is no longer mined with a single or multiple computer systems. As discussed in the bitcoin sections there are several ASIC (Application Specific Integrated Circuits).

Often people and experts asks me about trading in bitcoin and they also wonder that if they can mint some really good money if they invest in the bitcoin. As a security expert and a consultant it is always difficult to answer these kinds of questions. Not simply because people trust my answers but simply because the cryptocurrency markets are thousand times more volatile than the stock exchanges around the world.

If you are a new investor then my suggestion is that you can think of buying Ethereum or Litecoin. Our suggestion is purely based on some of the fundamental reasons presented in this book and we have already made the case till now. For any kind of investment one prerequisite is to have an in depth study of the universe. There is tremendous resource available on Internet. It is strongly recommended to watch the market trends and read all the details about the cryptocurrency before investing. A separate list of websites and watch indexes are given in the appendix sections of this book. If you are new to the investments than we strongly recommend you to read a classical book, The Intelligent Investor written by Benjamin Graham. Though the book was written in old but the investment fundamentals mentioned in the book are the kind of archetypes which can be implemented to any investment scenarios including cryptocurrencies.

If you are not sure about the future of cryptocurrencies and are concerned about the security then probably you are a wise investor. The kind of scams happening around in India, it is really difficult to believe in the Indian Exchanges which are owned and operated by individuals with a small team to dupe the investors. Therefore we strongly recommend you should always buy a cryptocurrency from a reputed exchange which you can find by going it to the respective cryptocurrency website. A list of good verified international exchanges are also given in the Appendix Section of this book.

Faucets

Faucets is an interesting way to earn little extra cryptocurrency. Initially the system was created for the promotion of the newly launched cryptocurrency where in users have to do a mundane task of filling up a form or a entering a captcha. Literally there are hundreds of websites on internet that offers the fractions of cryptocurrencies as a reward for completing the task. The biggest database for faucets earning is Faucet Hub *https://faucethub.io*.

You can also access this website with the QR printed in the Appendix section of this book.

PART SEVEN

Appendix

APPENDIX-I: Important Websites

Service Name	Website
Bit Finex	*https://www.bitfinex.com/*
Cex.io	*https://cex.io/*
Blockchain Info	*https://blockchain.info/*
Local Bitcoins	*https://localBitcoins.com/*
Bit Stamp	*https://www.bitstamp.net/*
Bit Rex	*https://bittrex.com/*
Gemini	*https://gemini.com/*
Ether Delta	*https://etherdelta.com/*
Kraken	*https://www.kraken.com/*
CoinBase	*https://www.coinbase.com/*
Crytopia	*https://www.cryptopia.co.nz/*
Changelly	*https://changelly.com/*
Yo Bit	*https://yobit.net/en/*

Desktop Wallet Services

Arc Bit	*https://Bitcoin.org/en/wallets/desktop/windows/arcbit/*
Green Address	*https://Bitcoin.org/en/wallets/desktop/windows/greenaddress/*
Electrum	*https://Bitcoin.org/en/wallets/desktop/windows/electrum/*

Bither	*https://Bitcoin.org/en/wallets/desktop/windows/bither/*
Bitcoin Wallet	*https://Bitcoin.org/en/*
Bitcoin Knots	*https://Bitcoin.org/en/wallets/desktop/windows/Bitcoinknots/*
mSIGNA	*https://Bitcoin.org/en/wallets/desktop/windows/msigna/*

Web Wallet Services

Coin.Space	*https://Bitcoin.org/en/wallets/web/coinspace/*
Green Address	*https://Bitcoin.org/en/wallets/web/greenaddress/*
Bit Go	*https://Bitcoin.org/en/wallets/web/bitgo/*

Hardware & Mobile Wallets (M-Mobile; H-Hardware)

Ledger Nano S (H)	*https://Bitcoin.org/en/wallets/hardware/ledgernanos/*
Mycelium (M)	*https://Bitcoin.org/en/wallets/mobile/android/mycelium/*
Trezor (H)	*https://Bitcoin.org/en/wallets/hardware/trezor/*
KeepKey (H)	*https://Bitcoin.org/en/wallets/hardware/keepkey/*
Simple Bitcoin Wallet (M)	*https://Bitcoin.org/en/wallets/mobile/android/simpleBitcoinwallet/*
Bitcoin Wallet (M)	*https://Bitcoin.org/en/wallets/mobile/android/Bitcoinwallet/*
Digital Bitbox (H)	*https://Bitcoin.org/en/wallets/hardware/digitalbitbox/*
Electrum (M)	*https://Bitcoin.org/en/wallets/mobile/android/electrum/*
Airbitz Bitcoin Wallet (M)	*https://Bitcoin.org/en/wallets/mobile/android/airbitzwallet/*

Here are some of the important International platforms to trade in Cryptocurrency Market specially Bitcoin. Both of these are authentic reliable trading platform used by millions of users for trade.

Plus 500	*https://www.plus500.co.uk/*
Ava Trade	*https://www.avatrade.com/*

Service Name	*Website*
Coin Dance	*https://coin.dance/*
Bit Info Charts	*https://bitinfocharts.com/Bitcoin/*
Coin Desk	*https://www.coindesk.com/*
Statista	*https://www.statista.com/topics/2308/bitcoin/*
Bitcoin Ticker	*http://Bitcointicker.co/*
Woo Bull Charts	*http://charts.woobull.com/bitcoin-volatility/*
Bit Vol	*https://bitvol.info/*
Coin Market Cap	*https://coinmarketcap.com/*
Coin Tracking	*https://cointracking.info/*
Blockonomics	*https://www.blockonomics.co/*

APPENDIX-II: White Paper Satoshi Nakamoto Bitcoin A Peer-to-Peer Electronic Cash System

Abstract. A purely peer-to-peer version of electronic cash would allow online payments to be sent directly from one party to another without going through a financial institution. Digital signatures provide part of the solution, but the main benefits are lost if a trusted third party is still required to prevent double-spending. We propose a solution to the double-spending problem using a peer-to-peer network. The network timestamps transactions by hashing them into an ongoing chain of hash-based proof-of-work, forming a record that cannot be changed without redoing the proof-of-work. The longest chain not only serves as proof of the sequence of events witnessed, but proof that it came from the largest pool of CPU power. As long as a majority of CPU power is controlled by nodes that are not cooperating to attack the network, they'll generate the longest chain and outpace attackers. The network itself requires minimal structure. Messages are broadcast on a best effort basis, and nodes can leave and rejoin the network at will, accepting the longest proof-of-work chain as proof of what happened while they were gone.

1. Introduction

Commerce on the Internet has come to rely almost exclusively on financial institutions serving as trusted third parties to process electronic payments. While the system works well enough for most transactions, it still suffers from the inherent weaknesses of the trust based model. Completely non-reversible transactions are not really possible, since financial institutions cannot avoid mediating disputes. The cost of mediation increases transaction costs, limiting the minimum practical transaction size and cutting off the possibility for small casual transactions, and there is a broader cost in the loss of ability to make non-reversible payments for non- reversible services. With the possibility of reversal, the need for trust spreads. Merchants must be wary of their customers, hassling them for more information than they would otherwise need. A certain percentage of fraud is accepted as unavoidable. These costs and payment uncertainties can be avoided in person by using physical currency, but no mechanism exists to make payments over a communications channel without a trusted party.

What is needed is an electronic payment system based on cryptographic proof instead of trust, allowing any two willing parties to transact directly with each other without the need for a trusted third party. Transactions that are computationally impractical to reverse would protect sellers from fraud, and routine escrow mechanisms could easily be implemented to protect buyers. In this paper, we propose a solution to the double-spending problem using a peer-to-peer distributed timestamp server to generate computational proof of the chronological order of transactions. The system is secure as long as honest nodes collectively control more CPU power than any cooperating group of attacker nodes.

2. Transactions

We define an electronic coin as a chain of digital signatures. Each owner transfers the coin to the next by digitally signing a hash of the previous transaction and the public key of the next owner and adding these to the end of the coin. A payee can verify the signatures to verify the chain of ownership.

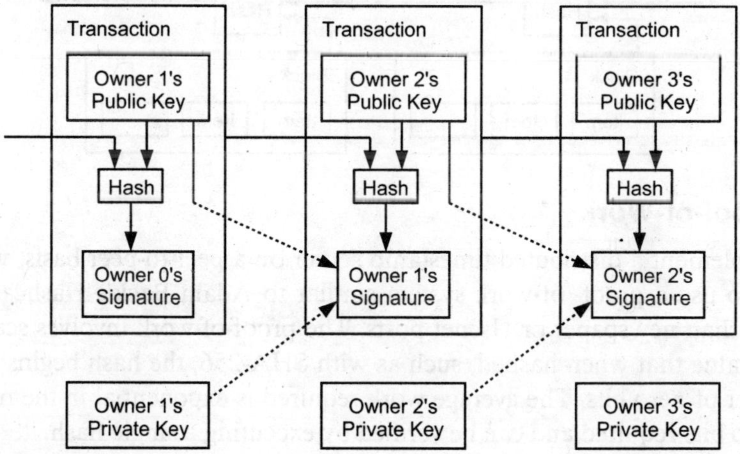

The problem of course is the payee can't verify that one of the owners did not double-spend the coin. A common solution is to introduce a trusted central authority, or mint, that checks every transaction for double spending. After each transaction, the coin must be returned to the mint to issue a new coin, and only coins issued directly from the mint are trusted not to be double-spent. The problem with this solution is that the fate of the entire money system depends on the company running the mint, with every transaction having to go through them, just like a bank.

We need a way for the payee to know that the previous owners did not sign any earlier transactions. For our purposes, the earliest transaction is the one that counts, so we don't care about later attempts to double-spend. The only way to confirm the absence of a transaction is to be aware of all transactions. In the mint based model, the mint was aware of all transactions and decided which arrived first. To accomplish this without a trusted party, transactions must be publicly announced [1], and we need a system for participants to agree on a single history of the order in which they were received. The payee needs proof that at the time of each transaction, the majority of nodes agreed it was the first received.

3. Timestamp Server

The solution we propose begins with a timestamp server. A timestamp server works by taking a hash of a block of items to be timestamped and widely publishing the hash, such as in a newspaper or Usenet post [2-5]. The timestamp proves that the data must have existed at the time, obviously, in order to get into the hash. Each timestamp includes the previous timestamp in its hash, forming a chain, with each additional timestamp reinforcing the ones before it.

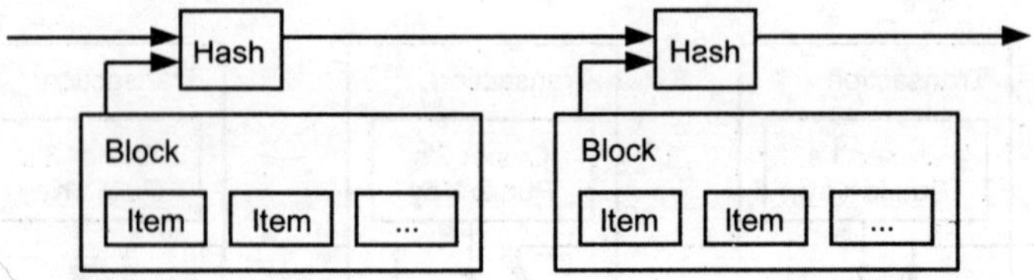

4. Proof-of-Work

To implement a distributed timestamp server on a peer-to-peer basis, we will need to use a proof- of-work system similar to Adam Back's Hashcash [6], rather than newspaper or Usenet posts. The proof-of-work involves scanning for a value that when hashed, such as with SHA-256, the hash begins with a number of zero bits. The average work required is exponential in the number of zero bits required and can be verified by executing a single hash.

For our timestamp network, we implement the proof-of-work by incrementing a nonce in the block until a value is found that gives the block's hash the required zero bits. Once the CPU effort has been expended to make it satisfy the proof-of-work, the block cannot be changed without redoing the work. As later blocks are chained after it, the work to change the block would include redoing all the blocks after it.

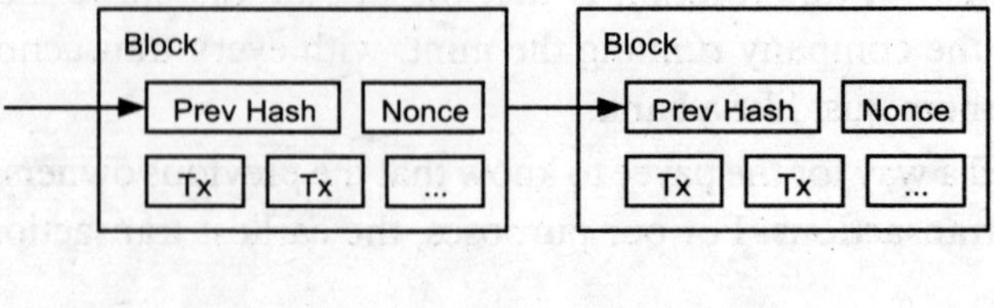

The proof-of-work also solves the problem of determining representation in majority decision making. If the majority were based on one-IP-address-one-vote, it could be subverted by anyone able to allocate many IPs. Proof-of-work is essentially one-CPU-one-vote. The majority decision is represented by the longest chain, which has the greatest proof-of-work effort invested in it. If a majority of CPU power is controlled by honest nodes, the honest chain will grow the fastest and outpace any competing chains. To modify a past block, an attacker would have to redo the proof-of-work of the block and all blocks after it and then catch up with and surpass the work of the honest nodes. We will show later that the probability of a slower attacker catching up diminishes exponentially as subsequent blocks are added.

To compensate for increasing hardware speed and varying interest in running nodes over time, the proof-of-work difficulty is determined by a moving average targeting an average number of blocks per hour. If they're generated too fast, the difficulty increases.

5. Network

The steps to run the network are as follows:

1. New transactions are broadcast to all nodes.
2. Each node collects new transactions into a block.
3. Each node works on finding a difficult proof-of-work for its block.
4. When a node finds a proof-of-work, it broadcasts the block to all nodes.
5. Nodes accept the block only if all transactions in it are valid and not already spent.
6. Nodes express their acceptance of the block by working on creating the next block in the chain, using the hash of the accepted block as the previous hash.

Nodes always consider the longest chain to be the correct one and will keep working on extending it. If two nodes broadcast different versions of the next block simultaneously, some nodes may receive one or the other first. In that case, they work on the first one they received, but save the other branch in case it becomes longer. The tie will be broken when the next proof- of-work is found and one branch becomes longer; the nodes that were working on the other branch will then switch to the longer one.

New transaction broadcasts do not necessarily need to reach all nodes. As long as they reach many nodes, they will get into a block before long. Block broadcasts are also tolerant of dropped messages. If a node does not receive a block, it will request it when it receives the next block and realizes it missed one.

6. Incentive

By convention, the first transaction in a block is a special transaction that starts a new coin owned by the creator of the block. This adds an incentive for nodes to support the network, and provides a way to initially distribute coins into circulation, since there is no central authority to issue them. The steady addition of a constant of amount of new coins is analogous to gold miners expending resources to add gold to circulation. In our case, it is CPU time and electricity that is expended.

The incentive can also be funded with transaction fees. If the output value of a transaction is less than its input value, the difference is a transaction fee that is added to the incentive value of the block containing the transaction. Once a predetermined number of coins have entered circulation, the incentive can transition entirely to transaction fees and be completely inflation free.

The incentive may help encourage nodes to stay honest. If a greedy attacker is able to assemble more CPU power than all the honest nodes, he would have to choose between using it to defraud people by stealing back his payments, or using it to generate new coins. He ought to find it more profitable to play by the rules, such rules that favour him with more new coins than everyone else combined, than to undermine the system and the validity of his own wealth.

7. Reclaiming Disk Space

Once the latest transaction in a coin is buried under enough blocks, the spent transactions before it can be discarded to save disk space. To facilitate this without breaking the block's hash, transactions are hashed in a Merkle Tree [7][2][5], with only the root included in the block's hash. Old blocks can then be compacted by stubbing off branches of the tree. The interior hashes do not need to be stored.

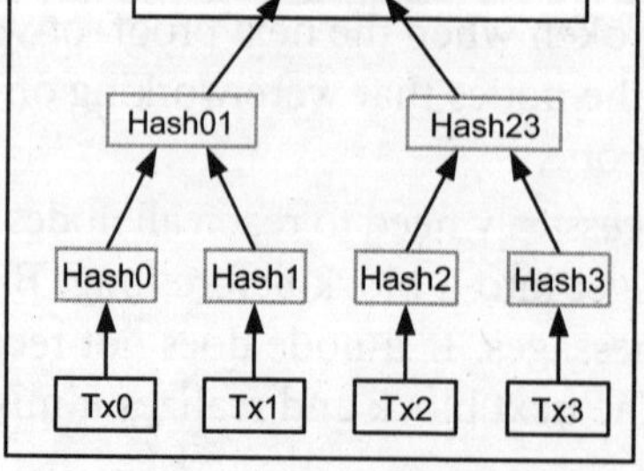

Transactions Hashed in a Merkle Tree

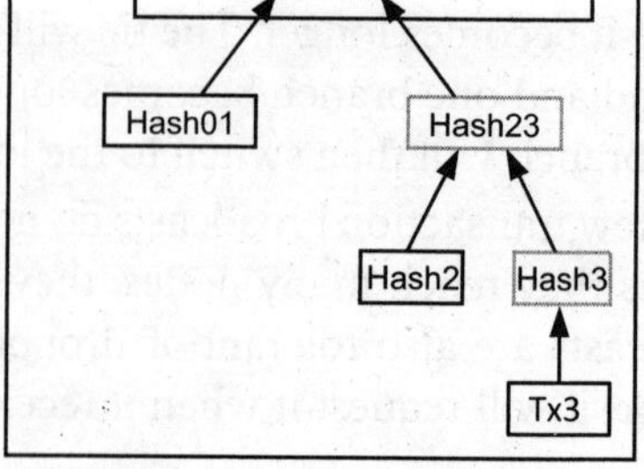

After Pruning Tx0-2 from the Block

A block header with no transactions would be about 80 bytes. If we suppose blocks are generated every 10 minutes, 80 bytes * 6 * 24 * 365 = 4.2MB per year. With computer systems typically selling with 2GB of RAM as of 2008, and Moore's Law predicting current growth of 1.2GB per year, storage should not be a problem even if the block headers must be kept in memory.

8. Simplified Payment Verification

It is possible to verify payments without running a full network node. A user only needs to keep a copy of the block headers of the longest proof-of-work chain, which he can get by querying network nodes until he's convinced he has the longest chain, and obtain the Merkle branch linking the transaction to the block it's timestamped in. He can't check the transaction for himself, but by linking it to a place in the chain, he can see that a network node has accepted it, and blocks added after it further confirm the network has accepted it.

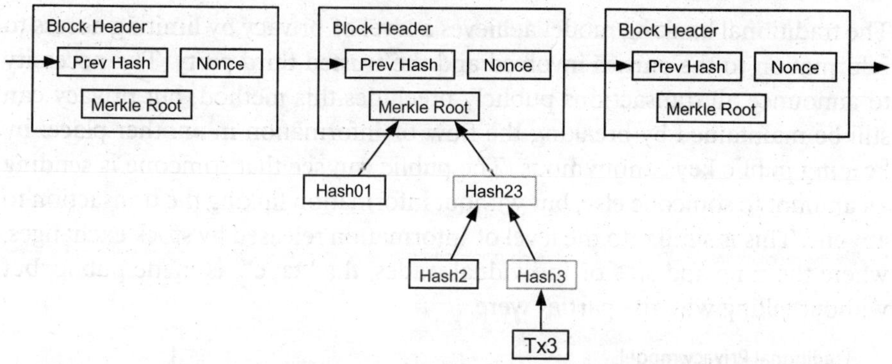

As such, the verification is reliable as long as honest nodes control the network, but is more vulnerable if the network is overpowered by an attacker. While network nodes can verify transactions for themselves, the simplified method can be fooled by an attacker's fabricated transactions for as long as the attacker can continue to overpower the network. One strategy to protect against this would be to accept alerts from network nodes when they detect an invalid block, prompting the user's software to download the full block and alerted transactions to confirm the inconsistency. Businesses that receive frequent payments will probably still want to run their own nodes for more independent security and quicker verification.

9. Combining and Splitting Value

Although it would be possible to handle coins individually, it would be unwieldy to make a separate transaction for every cent in a transfer. To allow value to be split and combined, transactions contain multiple inputs and outputs. Normally there will be either a single input from a larger previous transaction or multiple inputs combining smaller amounts, and at most two outputs: one for the payment, and one returning the change, if any, back to the sender.

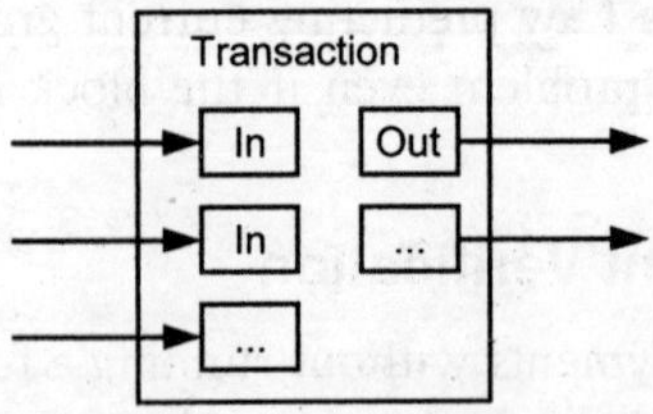

It should be noted that fan-out, where a transaction depends on several transactions, and those transactions depend on many more, is not a problem here. There is never the need to extract a complete standalone copy of a transaction's history.

10. Privacy

The traditional banking model achieves a level of privacy by limiting access to information to the parties involved and the trusted third party. The necessity to announce all transactions publicly precludes this method, but privacy can still be maintained by breaking the flow of information in another place: by keeping public keys anonymous. The public can see that someone is sending an amount to someone else, but without information linking the transaction to anyone. This is similar to the level of information released by stock exchanges, where the time and size of individual trades, the "tape", is made public, but without telling who the parties were.

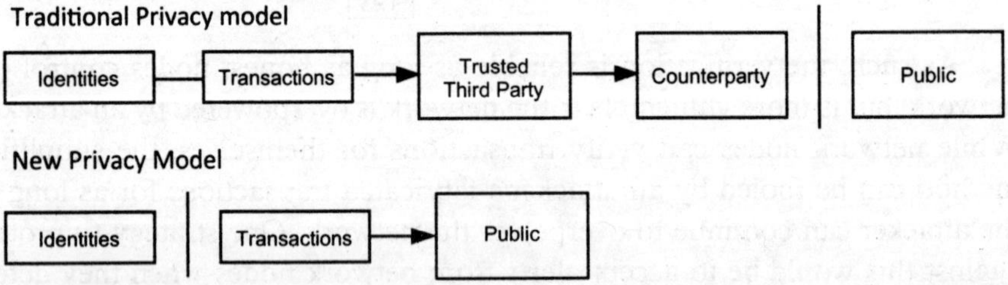

As an additional firewall, a new key pair should be used for each transaction to keep them from being linked to a common owner. Some linking is still unavoidable with multi-input transactions, which necessarily reveal that their inputs were owned by the same owner. The risk is that if the owner of a key is revealed, linking could reveal other transactions that belonged to the same owner.

11. Calculations

We consider the scenario of an attacker trying to generate an alternate chain faster than the honest chain. Even if this is accomplished, it does not throw the system open to arbitrary changes, such as creating value out of thin air or taking money that never belonged to the attacker. Nodes are not going to accept an invalid transaction as payment, and honest nodes will never accept a block containing them. An attacker can only try to change one of his own transactions to take back money he recently spent.

The race between the honest chain and an attacker chain can be characterized as a Binomial Random Walk. The success event is the honest chain being extended by one block, increasing its lead by +1, and the failure event is the attacker's chain being extended by one block, reducing the gap by –1.

The probability of an attacker catching up from a given deficit is analogous to a Gambler's Ruin problem. Suppose a gambler with unlimited credit starts at a deficit and plays potentially an infinite number of trials to try to reach breakeven. We can calculate the probability he ever reaches breakeven, or that an attacker ever catches up with the honest chain, as follows [8]:

p = probability an honest node finds the next block

q = probability the attacker finds the next block

q_z = probability the attacker will ever catch up from z blocks behind

$$q_z = \begin{Bmatrix} 1 & \textit{if } p \le q \\ (q/p)^z & \textit{f } p > q \end{Bmatrix}$$

Given our assumption that p > q, the probability drops exponentially as the number of blocks the attacker has to catch up with increases. With the odds against him, if he doesn't make a lucky lunge forward early on, his chances become vanishingly small as he falls further behind.

We now consider how long the recipient of a new transaction needs to wait before being sufficiently certain the sender can't change the transaction. We assume the sender is an attacker who wants to make the recipient believe he paid him for a while, then switch it to pay back to himself after some time has passed. The receiver will be alerted when that happens, but the sender hopes it will be too late.

The receiver generates a new key pair and gives the public key to the sender shortly before signing. This prevents the sender from preparing a chain of blocks ahead of time by working on it continuously until he is lucky enough to get far enough ahead, then executing the transaction at that moment. Once the transaction is sent, the dishonest sender starts working in secret on a parallel chain containing an alternate version of his transaction.

The recipient waits until the transaction has been added to a block and z blocks have been linked after it. He doesn't know the exact amount of progress the attacker has made, but assuming the honest blocks took the average expected time per block, the attacker's potential progress will be a Poisson distribution with expected value:

$$\lambda = z\frac{q}{p}$$

To get the probability the attacker could still catch up now, we multiply the Poisson density for each amount of progress he could have made by the probability he could catch up from that point:

$$\sum_{k=0}^{\infty} \frac{\lambda^k e^{-\lambda}}{k!} \cdot \begin{cases} (q/p)^{(z-k)} & \text{if } k \le z \\ 1 & \text{if } k > z \end{cases}$$

Rearranging to avoid summing the infinite tail of the distribution...

$$1 - \sum_{k=0}^{z} \frac{\lambda^k e^{-\lambda}}{k!}\left(1 - (q/p)^{(z-k)}\right)$$

Converting to C code...

```
#include <math.h>
double AttackerSuccessProbability(double q, int z)
{
double p = 1.0 - q;
double lambda = z * (q / p);
double sum = 1.0;
int i, k;
for (k = 0; k <= z; k++)
{
double poisson = exp(-lambda);
for (i = 1; i <= k; i++)
poisson *= lambda / i;
sum -= poisson * (1 - pow(q / p, z - k));
}
return sum;
}
```

Running some results, we can see the probability drop off exponentially with z.

```
q=0.1
z=0 P=1.0000000
z=1 P=0.2045873
z=2 P=0.0509779
```

```
z=3 P=0.0131722
z=4 P=0.0034552
z=5 P=0.0009137
z=6 P=0.0002428
z=7 P=0.0000647
z=8 P=0.0000173
z=9 P=0.0000046
z=10 P=0.0000012

q=0.3
z=0 P=1.0000000
z=5 P=0.1773523
z=10 P=0.0416605
z=15 P=0.0101008
z=20 P=0.0024804
z=25 P=0.0006132
z=30 P=0.0001522
z=35 P=0.0000379
z=40 P=0.0000095
z=45 P=0.0000024
z=50 P=0.0000006
```

12. Conclusion

We have proposed a system for electronic transactions without relying on trust. We started with the usual framework of coins made from digital signatures, which provides strong control of ownership, but is incomplete without a way to prevent double-spending. To solve this, we proposed a peer-to-peer network using proof-of-work to record a public history of transactions that quickly becomes computationally impractical for an attacker to change if honest nodes control a majority of CPU power. The network is robust in its unstructured simplicity. Nodes work all at once with little coordination. They do not need to be identified, since messages are not routed to any particular place and only need to be delivered on a best effort basis. Nodes can leave and rejoin the network at will, accepting the proof-of-work chain as proof of what happened while they were gone. They vote with their CPU power, expressing their acceptance of valid blocks by working on extending them and rejecting invalid blocks by refusing to work on them. Any needed rules and incentives can be enforced with this consensus mechanism.

References

1. W. Dai, "b-money," *http://www.weidai.com/bmoney.txt*, 1998.
2. H. Massias, X.S. Avila, and J.-J. Quisquater, "Design of a secure timestamping service with minimal trust requirements," In 20th Symposium on Information Theory in the Benelux, May 1999.
3. S. Haber, W.S. Stornetta, "How to time-stamp a digital document," In Journal of Cryptology, vol 3, no2, pages 99-111, 1991.
4. D. Bayer, S. Haber, W.S. Stornetta, "Improving the efficiency and reliability of digital time-stamping," In Sequences II: Methods in Communication, Security and Computer Science, pages 329-334, 1993.
5. S. Haber, W.S. Stornetta, "Secure names for bit-strings," In Proceedings of the 4th ACM Conference on Computer and Communications Security, pages 28-35, April 1997.
6. A. Back, "Hashcash - a denial of service counter-measure," *http://www.hashcash.org/papers/hashcash.pdf*, 2002.
7. R.C. Merkle, "Protocols for public key crypto systems," In Proc. 1980 Symposium on Security and Privacy, IEEE Computer Society, pages 122-133, April 1980.
8. W. Feller, "An introduction to probability theory and its applications," 1957.

APPENDIX-III: QR Codes

Here are some QR codes of some interesting available material on Internet. To watch this content you need to download QR Code scanner app from your Android or apple itunes Market. After installing a QR scanner scan the QR code to watch the listed content.

1. China's secret Bitcoin Mine.

2. How I build a Bitcoin Empire.

3. Blockchain Simplified

4. How Blockchain can Transform Economy.

5. Seven Minute Guide to Invest in Cryptocurrencies.

6. An Interesting perspective on why Crypto Market is crashing to ponder on.

7. List of some really interesting cryptocurrency pod casts.

8. Faucet Hub

APPENDIX-IV: Glossary

Address – A secure identifier marked by a unique string of characters that enables payments to an individual or entity via blockchain transactions. It usually requires a private key to exclusively access the funds. For example, bitcoin addresses are alphanumeric strings that begin with a 1 or 3; Ethereum addresses begin with '0x'.

Altcoin – A cryptocurrency or a category of cryptocurrencies that are an alternative to bitcoin. Many altcoins project themselves as better alternatives to bitcoin in various ways (e.g. more efficient, less expensive, etc.).

Bitcoin (BTC) – A type of cryptocurrency created by Satoshi Nakamoto in 2009. It was one of the first digital currencies that enabled instant P2P payments. Bitcoins are created through a process known as bitcoin mining that requires a massive amount of computing power. For more information, please see the bitcoin whitepaper.

Bitcoin Cash (BCH) – A type of cryptocurrency that was created in August 2017 and is essentially a clone of the Bitcoin blockchain but has increased block size capacity (from 1 MB to 8 MB) as a way to solve the scaling problem. For more information, please visit their official website.

Block – Refers to a collection of data related to transactions that are bundled together with a predetermized size and are processed for transaction verification and eventually becomes part of a blockchain.

Blockchain – A decentralized, digital ledger where transactions made in bitcoin or other cryptocurrencies are recorded chronologically and publicly. The block contains information that, once it goes into the blockchain, it becomes part of the permanent and immutable database, connecting to other blocks in the blockchain like the links in a chain.

Circulating supply – An approximation of the number of coins or tokens that are circulating in the public market. See also: Total Supply and Maximum Supply.

Cryptocurrency – A type of digital currency that is generally decentralized and uses cryptography (i.e. data is converted into a format that is unreadable for unauthorized users) for added security, making it difficult to counterfeit or manipulate.

Dash – A type of cryptocurrency based on bitcoin software but has anonymity features that makes it impossible to trace transactions to an individual and other capabilities. It was created by Evan Duffield in 2014 and was previously known as XCoin (XCO) and Darkcoin. For more information, visit the official website for DASH.

Decentralized – A state where there is no central control, power or function, or in reference to infrastructure, no central point of failure. See Vitalik Buterin's definition of decentralization.

Decentralized applications (dApps) – A type of software program that runs on a decentralized P2P network rather than on a single computer. Although similar, it differs from smart contracts as it can have any number of participants on all sides of the market and it does not have to be financial. Ethereum is a popular development platform for creating dApps. For more information, see Vitalik Buterin's terminology guide.

Distributed consensus – Collective agreement by various computers in a network and allows it to work in a decentralized, P2P manner without the need of central authority to deter dishonest network participants.

ERC–20 – A type of token standard for Ethereum which ensures the tokens perform in a predictable way. This allows the tokens to be easily exchangeable and able to work immediately with decentralized applications that also use the ERC–20 standard. Most tokens released through ICOsare compliant with the ERC–20 standard.

Ether (ETH) – A type of cryptocurrency that is used for operating the Ethereum platform and is used to pay for transaction fees and computational tasks. In the platform, transaction fees are measured based on the gas limit and gas price and ultimately paid for in Ether. For more information, see the Ethereum Foundation's official definition.

Ethereum – An open source, decentralized platform based on blockchain technology created by Vitalik Buterin in 2013. It runs smart contracts on a custom built blockchain that allows developers to create markets, store registries of debts, and so on. For more information, please visit the Ethereum Foundation website or read their whitepaper.

Ethereum Classic (ETC) – A type of cryptocurrency that is a continuation of the original Ethereum blockchain following the DAO attack in June 2016. Ethereum is essentially a hard fork of the blockchain that was formed to refund the money that was siphoned during the attack (around $50 million). Ethereum Classic assumes no hard fork occurred and is supported by those who believe in complete immutability of the blockchain. For more information, visit the website for Ethereum Classic.

Fiat money – Refers to currencies that have minimal or no intrinsic value themselves (i.e. they are not backed by commodities like gold or silver) but are defined as legal tender by the government, such as paper bills and coins.

Flipping – A type of investment strategy (popular in real estate investing) where you buy something with the goal of reselling for a profit later, usually in a short period of time. In the context of ICOs, flipping refers to the strategy of investing in tokens before they are listed on the exchanges and reselling them for a profit when they are trading in the secondary market.

FOMO – An acronym that stands for 'fear of missing out' and in the context of investing, refers to the feeling of apprehension for missing out on a potentially profitable investment opportunity and regretting it later.

FUD – An acronym that stands for fear, uncertainty and doubt. It is a strategy to influence perception by spreading negative, misleading or false information about something, as opposed to reasoned criticism.

Gas limit – A term used in the Ethereum platform that refers to the maximum amount of units of gas the user is willing to spend on a transaction. The transaction must have enough gas to cover the computational resources needed to execute the code. All unused gas is refunded at the end of the transaction.

Gas price – A term used in the Ethereum platform that refers to the price you are willing to pay for a transaction. Setting a higher gas price will make miners more incentivized to prioritize and validate that particular transaction ahead of those set with a lower gas price. Gas prices are typically denominated in Gwei. For more information on the various ether denominations, see this documentation.

Genesis block – The first block of data that is processed and validated to form a new blockchain, often referred to as block 0 or block 1.

Hard cap – The maximum amount that an ICO will be raising. If an ICO reaches its hard cap, they will stop collecting any more funds. See also: soft cap.

HODL – A type of passive investment strategy where you hold an investment for a long period of time, regardless of market volatility. The term was made famous by a typo made in a Bitcoin Forum. Also referred to as 'buy and hold' or 'hold on for dear life'.

Initial coin offering (ICO) – An unregulated means by which a cryptocurrency venture, typically early stage, can raise money from supporters by issuing tokens. It is often referred to as a crowdsale as ICO participants may potentially earn a return on their investments (as opposed to crowdfunding, where supporters donate money to a project or cause). Ethereum is currently the most popular platform for launching ICOs.

IOTA (MIOTA) – Refers to the cryptocurrency and the name of an open source distributed ledger founded in 2015 that does not use blockchain (it uses a new distributed ledger called the Tangle). It offers features such as zero fees, scalability, fast and secure transactions, and so on. It is focused on the Internet of Things. For more information, visit the official website and the FAQs page for IOTA.

Lightning Network – A low latency, off chain P2P system for making micropayments of cryptocurrencies. It offers features such as instant payments, scalability, low cost and cross–chain functionality. Participants do not have to make individual transactions public on the blockchain and security is enforced by smart contracts. For more information, visit the official website or the whitepaper.

Litecoin (LTC) – A type of cryptocurrency that was created by former Google employee Charlie Lee in 2011. It offers features such as Segregated Witness and the Lightning Network which allows for faster processing at lower cost. For more information, visit the Litecoin website.

Market capitalization (market cap) – The market value of a company, market or sector at a point in time commonly used to rank relative size. In equities, it refers to the total market value of a company's outstanding shares. In cryptocurrency investing, it refers to either price multiplied by the circulating supply (i.e. free float market cap) or price multiplied by the total supply (i.e. fully diluted market cap).

Maximum supply – An approximation of the maximum number of coins or tokens that will ever exist for a cryptocurrency or crypto asset. See also: circulating supply and total supply.

Mining – A process where transactions are verified and added to a blockchain. It is also the process where new bitcoins or certain altcoins are created. In theory, anyone with the necessary hardware and access to the internet can be a miner and earn income, but the cost of industrial hardware and electricity has limited mining for bitcoins and certain altcoins today to large–scale operations.

Monero (XMR) – A type of cryptocurrency created in 2014 that is focused on privacy and scalability, and runs on platforms like Windows, Mac, Linux and Android. Transactions on Monero are designed to be untraceable to any particular user or real world identity. For more information, please visit the Monero website.

NEM (XEM) – Refers to the cryptocurrency and the name of a platform for management of a variety of assets, including currencies, supply chains, ownership records, etc. It offers additional features to blockchain technology such as multi–signature accounts, encrypted messaging, etc. For more information, please visit their official website.

NEO – Refers to the cryptocurrency and the name of a China's first open source blockchain that was founded in 2014 by Da Hongfei. It is similar to Ethereum in its ability to execute smart contracts or dApps but has some technical differences such as coding language compatibility. For more information, visit their official website.

Pre–sale – A sale that takes place before an ICO is made available to the general public to participate.

Proof of Stake (PoS) – An algorithm that rewards participants that solves difficult cryptographic puzzles to achieve distributed consensus. Unlike proof of work or PoW, a person can validate transactions and create new blocks based on their individual wealth (i.e. stake) such as the total number of coins owned. One of the key advantages that PoS has over PoW is lower energy consumption.

Proof of Work (PoW) – An algorithm that rewards the first person that solves a computational problem (i.e. mining) to achieve distributed consensus. Miners compete to solve difficult cryptographic puzzles in order to add the next block on the blockchain. It prevents spam and cyber attacks such as DDoS as it requires work (i.e. processing time) from the service requester.

Pump and dump scheme – A scheme in which the development team (or short–term traders) hypes up a project without fundamental basis in order to pump up the price of the tokens temporarily and then sells their holdings immediately after launch to earn a profit. See the US SEC's investor alerton pump and dump schemes.

Ripple (XRP) – Refers to the cryptocurrency and the name of an open source payment platform where the cryptocurrency (Ripple or XRP) can be transferred. The vision for the platform is to enable real–time global payments anywhere around the world. The Ripple payment protocol was built by OpenCoin which was founded in 2012. For more information, visit Ripple's official website.

Segregated Witness (SegWit) – The process where the block size limit on a blockchain is increased by removing digital signature data and moving it to the end of a transaction to free up capacity. Transactions are essentially split (or 'segregated'), into two segments: the original data segment and the signature (or 'witness') segment.

Smart contracts – An automated mechanism involving two or more parties where digital assets are put in and redistributed at a later date based on some preset formula and triggering event. The contract can run as programmed without any downtime, censorship, fraud or third party interference. For more information, see Vitalik Buterin's terminology guide.

Soft cap – Generally refers to the minimum amount that an initial coin offering (ICO) needs to raise. If the ICO is unable to raise that amount, it may be cancelled and the collected funds returned to participants. See also: hard cap.

Token – Crypto tokens enable the creation of open, decentralized networks, and provides a way to incentivize participants in the network (with both network growth and token appreciation). This innovation, made popular with the introduction of Ethereum, has given rise to a wave of token networks (e.g. prediction markets, content creation networks, etc.) and token pre–sales, or ICOs.

Total supply – The total number of coins or tokens that are in existence, including those circulating in the public market and those that are locked or reserved. See also: maximum supply and total supply.

Wallet – A store of digital assets such as cryptocurrencies, analogous to a digital bank account. Crypto wallets can be divided into two categories: hosted wallets (e.g. wallets store on exchanges or third–party servers) and cold wallets (e.g. hardware wallets such as the Ledger Nano S, paper wallets and desktop wallets).

Whitelist – A list of registered and approved participants that are given exclusive access to contribute to an ICO or a pre–sale.

Whitepaper – An informational document that generally informs readers on the philosophy, objectives and technology of a project or initiative. Whitepapers are often provided before the launch of a new coin or token.